Advances in Science, Technology & Innovation

IEREK Interdisciplinary Series for Sustainable Development

Editorial Board

Anna Laura Pisello, Department of Engineering, University of Perugia, Italy

Dean Hawkes, University of Cambridge, Cambridge, UK

Hocine Bougdah, University for the Creative Arts, Farnham, UK

Federica Rosso, Sapienza University of Rome, Rome, Italy

Hassan Abdalla, University of East London, London, UK

Sofia-Natalia Boemi, Aristotle University of Thessaloniki, Greece

Nabil Mohareb, Faculty of Architecture—Design and Built Environment, Beirut Arab University, Beirut, Lebanon

Saleh Mesbah Elkaffas, Arab Academy for Science, Technology and Maritime Transport, Cairo, Egypt

Emmanuel Bozonnet, University of La Rochelle, La Rochelle, France

Gloria Pignatta, University of Perugia, Italy

Yasser Mahgoub, Qatar University, Qatar

Luciano De Bonis, University of Molise, Italy

Stella Kostopoulou, Regional and Tourism Development, University of Thessaloniki, Thessaloniki, Greece

Biswajeet Pradhan, Faculty of Engineering and IT, University of Technology Sydney, Sydney, Australia

Md. Abdul Mannan, Universiti Malaysia Sarawak, Malaysia

Chaham Alalouch, Sultan Qaboos University, Muscat, Oman

Iman O. Gawad, Helwan University, Helwan, Egypt

Anand Nayyar, Graduate School, Duy Tan University, Da Nang, Vietnam

Series Editor

Mourad Amer, International Experts for Research Enrichment and Knowledge Exchange (IEREK), Cairo, Egypt

AF780945

Advances in Science, Technology & Innovation (ASTI) is a series of peer-reviewed books based on important emerging research that redefines the current disciplinary boundaries in science, technology and innovation (STI) in order to develop integrated concepts for sustainable development. It not only discusses the progress made towards securing more resources, allocating smarter solutions, and rebalancing the relationship between nature and people, but also provides in-depth insights from comprehensive research that addresses the **17 sustainable development goals (SDGs)** as set out by the UN for 2030.

The series draws on the best research papers from various IEREK and other international conferences to promote the creation and development of viable solutions for a **sustainable future and a positive societal** transformation with the help of integrated and innovative science-based approaches. Including interdisciplinary contributions, it presents innovative approaches and highlights how they can best support both economic and sustainable development, through better use of data, more effective institutions, and global, local and individual action, for the welfare of all societies.

The series particularly features conceptual and empirical contributions from various interrelated fields of science, technology and innovation, with an emphasis on digital transformation, that focus on providing practical solutions to **ensure food, water and energy security to achieve the SDGs.** It also presents new case studies offering concrete examples of how to resolve sustainable urbanization and environmental issues in different regions of the world.

The series is intended for professionals in research and teaching, consultancies and industry, and government and international organizations. Published in collaboration with IEREK, the Springer ASTI series will acquaint readers with essential new studies in STI for sustainable development.

ASTI series has now been accepted for Scopus (September 2020). All content published in this series will start appearing on the Scopus site in early 2021.

Asma Salman · Assem Tharwat
Editors

ICT for Engineering & Critical Infrastructures

Proceedings of the 3rd American University in the Emirates International Research Conference, AUEIRC'20—Dubai, UAE 2020

Springer

Editors
Asma Salman
College of Business Administration
American University in the Emirates (AUE)
Dubai, United Arab Emirates

Assem Tharwat
American University in the Emirates (AUE)
Dubai, United Arab Emirates

ISSN 2522-8714 ISSN 2522-8722 (electronic)
Advances in Science, Technology & Innovation
ISBN 978-3-031-49311-9 ISBN 978-3-031-49309-6 (eBook)
https://doi.org/10.1007/978-3-031-49309-6

© The Editor(s) (if applicable) and The Author(s), under exclusive license to Springer Nature Switzerland AG 2024, corrected publication 2024

This work is subject to copyright. All rights are solely and exclusively licensed by the Publisher, whether the whole or part of the material is concerned, specifically the rights of translation, reprinting, reuse of illustrations, recitation, broadcasting, reproduction on microfilms or in any other physical way, and transmission or information storage and retrieval, electronic adaptation, computer software, or by similar or dissimilar methodology now known or hereafter developed.
The use of general descriptive names, registered names, trademarks, service marks, etc. in this publication does not imply, even in the absence of a specific statement, that such names are exempt from the relevant protective laws and regulations and therefore free for general use.
The publisher, the authors, and the editors are safe to assume that the advice and information in this book are believed to be true and accurate at the date of publication. Neither the publisher nor the authors or the editors give a warranty, expressed or implied, with respect to the material contained herein or for any errors or omissions that may have been made. The publisher remains neutral with regard to jurisdictional claims in published maps and institutional affiliations.

This Springer imprint is published by the registered company Springer Nature Switzerland AG
The registered company address is: Gewerbestrasse 11, 6330 Cham, Switzerland

Paper in this product is recyclable.

Preface

The 3rd American University in the Emirates International Research Conference (AUEIRC'20) under the theme "Transition to Knowledge Economy: Challenges, Smart Opportunities and Innovation" brought together academics, researchers, and practitioners under one platform with the aim of sharing ideas and expertise in the most pressing challenges that the world has witnessed. Under the Patronage of H.H. Sheikh Hamdan Bin Rashid Al Maktoum, Deputy Ruler of Dubai and Minister of Finance, United Arab Emirates (UAE), the 3rd AUEIRC 2020 was held between August 8 and 11 2020. The proceedings will be published in the ***Transition to Knowledge Economy: Challenges, Smart Opportunities, and Innovation*** book series of Springer.

As the first research conference to be conducted virtually in the Middle East, covering vital sectors of the economy and the impact of COVID-19, this conference was a testimony that digital transformation indeed leads to the continuity of exchange of knowledge. It warranted a vision, where the academics, practitioners, and policymakers from the region and across the globe engaged in a dialogue to discuss some of the most pressing issues in knowledge economy and the pandemic that has gripped the world, while focusing on the application side of the research rather than just the theoretical ones.

The scope of the conference included eight main themes, namely COVID-19 Challenges, Entrepreneurship, Computer and Advanced Technology, Education Industry, Security and Global Studies, Law, Integrated Media, and Design Industry. The 3rd AUEIRC 2020 witnessed research paper presentations from 101 presenters in 18 different sessions under these eight tracks. The conference boasted of imminent speakers from the industry and academia covering pertinent issues and offering plausible solutions. It had seven keynote sessions, six interactive workshops, talks from 20 experts from the industry, and participation from over 25 countries during the 4-day conference. Each speaker brought with them a wealth of knowledge and concluded with a range of questions and discussions from the audience and the panels. Worthy speakers included: H.E. Mr. Mirza Al Sayegh, Director, Office of H.H. Sheikh Hamden Bin Rashid Al Maktoum (United Arab Emirates); Major Gen. Dr. Ahmed Nasser Al Raisi, General Inspector of the Ministry of Interior (United Arab Emirates); Prof. Suzanne Trager Ortega, President of the Council of Graduate Schools (USA); H.E. Dr. Dena Assaf, United Nations Resident Coordinator for UAE; and H.E. Jamal Al Jarwan, Secretary General-UAE International Investors Council (United Arab Emirates).

The International Scientific Committee comprised of over 40 international experts in various fields as per the themes of the conference. The panels were divided based on tracks, and all papers were presented in 18 thematic sessions. In an aim to bridge the gap between theory and practice, each session was organized to have an academic and an industry representative as a chair and/or co-chair. This enhanced the feedback and reflected discussions from a well-rounded perspective. Sessions were designed to start with the paper presentations, and then the floor was opened for a healthy exchange of feedback. A double-blind peer-review process enabled 50 full papers to be accepted for publication (in five edited volumes) by Springer.

This volume supports the deployment of ICT augmentation for engineering critical infrastructures, offers revolutionary ICT solutions for smart networking, and builds on research in the area of cybersecurity and forensic innovation for infrastructures.

On behalf of the AUEIRC'20 Steering Committee, we would like to thank all the referees, track chairs, and paper authors. Special thanks to Prof. Muthanna G. Abdul Razzaq, President, and CEO American University in the Emirates (AUE) and AUEIRC'20 General Chair who contributed all resources at his disposal to ensure the conference meets the standard of excellence. We would also like to thank Major Gen. Dr. Ahmed Nasser Al Raisi, General Inspector of the Ministry of Interior, United Arab Emirates and Chairman Board of Trustees (AUE) for his valuable support. Special gratitude to members of the conference steering committee for their hard work, dedication, and continuous support throughout the preparation and implementation of this virtual conference. Moreover, we are grateful to the event management, information technology department, auxiliary services, media, protocol teams as well as faculty and staff members from different committees for their support in organizing the conference and ensuring its success.

Dubai, United Arab Emirates

Prof. Asma Salman
asma.salman@aue.ae
Prof. Assem Tharwat
assem.tharwat@aue.ae

About This Book

Advanced computing methods and technologies are changing the way engineers interact with the information of infrastructure. A new emerging engineering discipline integrating Information Technology (IT) with a variety of Engineering disciplines—which portrays its emphasis on Knowledge and Computational Engineering or rather 'Software'—is known as *Engineering Informatics*. Interdisciplinary in nature, its application relies on advanced information and Information Communication Technologies (ICTs), as well as a collaborative effort, to achieve social, economic, and environmental goals.

That said, Information and communication Technologies play an integral role in our world and rely on computing, informatics, networking, and cybersecurity, all of which have proven essential in today's digital and knowledge economy era especially following the COVID-19 pandemic. The four parts of the book aims to showcase research and developments in ICTs for engineering and the increasing gravity of security in cyberspace and Critical Infrastructures. It also provides revolutionary ICT solutions for networking and covers Cyber security and forensic innovation for Critical infrastructure systems.

The book presents selected papers submitted to the 3rd American University in the Emirates International Research Conference (AUEIRC'20), which brought together academics, researchers, and practitioners under one platform with the aim of sharing ideas and expertise in the most pressing challenges that the world has witnessed. Under the Patronage of H. H. Sheikh Hamdan Bin Rashid Al Maktoum, Deputy Ruler of Dubai and Minister of Finance, United Arab Emirates (UAE), the 3rd AUEIRC 2020, was held between August 8th–11th 2020.

As one of the earliest adopters of virtual research conferencing in the Middle East, covering vital sectors of the economy and the impact of COVID-19, this conference was a testimony that digital transformation indeed leads to the continuity of exchange of knowledge. It warranted a vision, where the academics, practitioners, and policymakers from the region and across the globe engaged in a dialogue to discuss some of the most pressing issues in Informatics Education, both in-light of and in-spite of the pandemic that has gripped the world, while focusing on the application side of the research rather than just the theoretical ones. This book will be useful for undergraduate and graduate students, researchers, and scholars in the fields of Computer Science and Engineering in addition to engineers, scientists, ICT managers.

Contents

Neurocontroller Design for Solar-Powered Wireless Network System

Waleed Al-Azzawi and Marwan Al-Akaidi

Abstract

Solar lighting system offers a clean environment and therefore able to continue for a long period. In this paper presented is a neural network predictive control technique for a solar-powered wireless networked control system. Solar wireless networked control systems model is created by using back-propagation. Adaptive learning rate approach is used to identify the stochastic time delays in back-propagation neural network. The performance of the controller is based on minimisation of the mean square error. The simulation results demonstrate that the proposed design methodologies can achieve the prescribed performance requirements.

Keywords

Controller · Predictive control · Wireless · Neural network

1 Introduction

The Neural Network Predictor Control (NNPC) controller that is implemented using the MATLAB Neural Network Toolbox software employs a neural network model of a physical plant to predict future plant performance. It has been shown that neural networks (NNs) have the capability to estimate virtually any function of attention to any level of accuracy under the assumption that the neural network is presented with sufficiently many hidden units. Based on this capability, NNs have been applied extensively in time series predictions (Pang and Liu 2010; Wang and Zhou 2007; Yi and Wang 2007; Al-Azzawi and Al-Akaidi 2012, 2020; Sauer and Fischer 2016; Elsersy et al. 2016). The main problem facing solar wireless networked control systems (SWNCSs) face is the network stochastic time delay, which can frequently degrade the performance of the SWNCS and even destabilise the system. Aiming to resolving this problem, a new model proposed for the SWNCSs, which is stimulated from a variable time sampling approach and applying predictive control techniques employing NN. The design demonstrates the construction of the predictive controller and the optimisation functions that are typically employed to update the control signal, then applies the NN method. Predictive control is characterised by achieving the prediction of future values via a model (Magdi 2014; Neumann 2016; Ploplys 2015).

In this paper, a new method is presented for SWNCS analysis and design based on TrueTime simulation tools by designing NNPC controller-based MSE performance predictive criterion. SWNCS is designed with specific communications and control parameters using TrueTime simulator tools. A NNPC which is capable of estimating and removing the effect of the delay times that occurs in the SWNCS is introduced. This can be achieved by assuming that stochastic time delays occurring in forward and feedback channels are predicted using a BPNN and a learning algorithm which adopts an adaptive learning rate approach. The NNPC controller will be able to enhance the QoS of SWNCS by removing the effect of time delays which occur in the forward and feedback channels of the SWNCS.

2 Problem Formulation

We assumed the configuration of that suppose the SWNCS as depicted, in Fig. 1, its physical plant is modelled by the following system:

The original version of the chapter has been revised: The author "Marwan Al-Akaidi" affiliation has been updated. A correction to the chapter can be found at https://doi.org/10.1007/978-3-031-49309-6_8

W. Al-Azzawi
Al Farahidi University, Baghdad, Iraq

M. Al-Akaidi (✉)
Wigwe University
Isiokpo, Nigeria
e-mail: mmalakaidi@gmail.com

© The Author(s), under exclusive license to Springer Nature Switzerland AG 2024, corrected publication 2024

A. Salman and A. Tharwat (eds.), *ICT for Engineering & Critical Infrastructures*,
Advances in Science, Technology & Innovation, https://doi.org/10.1007/978-3-031-49309-6_1

$$X(k+1) = AX(k) + Bu\left(k - \tau_k^{ca}\right) \quad (1a)$$

$$Y(k) = CX(k) \quad (1b)$$

where $X(k)$ is the state vector, $U(k)$ is the control input, $Y(k)$ is the output, A, B, C are system matrices with appropriate dimensions and τ_k^{ca} is a random delay from controller-to-actuator.

A NNPC based on BP controller with a learning algorithm adopting an adaptive learning rate approach such that the response of the closed SWNCS can follow a reference signal to get the required tracking control performance.

$$u(k) = k_1\left(\tau_k^{sc}, \tau_{k-\tau_k^{sc}-1}^{ca}\right)X_p\left(k - \tau_k^{sc}\right) + k_2\left(\tau_k^{sc}, \tau_{k-\tau_k^{sc}-1}^{ca}\right)X\left(k - \tau_k^{sc}\right) \quad (2)$$

Referring to the stochastic time delay τ_k^{ca}, the following SWNCS model can be achieved

$$X(k+1) = \tilde{A}X(k) + \tilde{B}U\left(k - \tau_k^{ca}\right) + \tilde{J}r(k) \quad (3a)$$

$$Y(k) = \tilde{C}X(k) \quad (3b)$$

where

$$X(k) = \left[x_r(k)^{\mathrm{T}} x(k)^{\mathrm{T}}\right]$$

$$\tilde{A} = \begin{bmatrix} A_r & 0 \\ 0 & A \end{bmatrix}$$

$$\tilde{B} = \begin{bmatrix} 0 \\ B \end{bmatrix}$$

$$\tilde{J} = \begin{bmatrix} B_r \\ 0 \end{bmatrix}$$

$$\tilde{C} = [-C_r C]$$

2.1 Neural Network Predictive Control (NNPC)

The controller than computes the control signal that will optimise plant performance over a specified future time horizon. This can be achieved by the following two steps:

Step 1 in model predictive control is to establish the neural network SWNCS model (system identification).

Step 2 the SWNCS model is employed by the controller to predict future performance. The first step of MPC is to train a NN to characterise the forward dynamics of the SWNC. The prediction error between the SWNCS output and the NN output is used as the NN training signal. The neural network model can be trained online in set mode using information collected from the operation of the SWNCS models.

$$a^1 = f\left(W^{1,1} e_p(t) + b^1\right) \quad (4a)$$

$$e_p(t+1) = f\left(W^{2,1} a^1 + b^2\right) \quad (4b)$$

where, $f(.)$ is a tangent hyperbolic function and is defined as:

$$f(x) = \frac{e^x - e^{-x}}{e^x + e^{-x}} \quad (5a)$$

$$\dot{f} = 1 - f^2(x) \quad (5b)$$

The back-propagation (BP) training algorithm.

The term back-propagation refers to the mode in which the gradient is calculated for nonlinear multilayer networks. There are a number of variations on the basic algorithm that are based on other optimisation methods, such as conjugate gradient and Newton methods (Yi and Wang 2007). The BP mathematical approach is summarised as:

$$w_{ji}^l(k+1) = w_{ji}^l(k) - \lambda \frac{\delta F(k)}{\delta w_{ji}^l(k)} \quad (6a)$$

$$b_j^l(k+1) = b_j^l(k) - \rho \frac{\delta F(k)}{\delta b_j^l(k)} \quad (6b)$$

where l is the layer number, $i = 1, 2, \ldots, \varepsilon_{l-1}$, and $j = 1, 2, \ldots, \varepsilon_l$, λ and ρ—are learning rates.

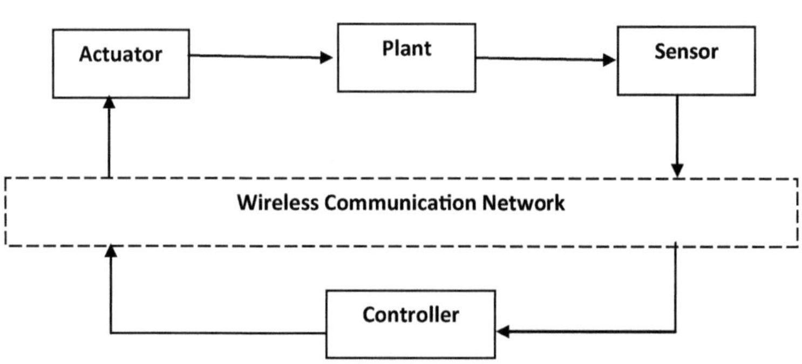

Fig. 1 SWNCS configuration

$F(k) = \frac{1}{\varepsilon_2}\sum_{j=1}^{\varepsilon_2} e_j^2(k)$, $e_j(k) = t_j(k) - y_{pj}^2(k)$ where t is the target vector and y_p is the output vector

$$\frac{\delta F(k)}{\delta x} = \begin{cases} -2e_j(k)a_i^1, x = w_{ji}^2 \\ -2e_j(k), x = b_j^2 \end{cases} \quad (7)$$

2.1.1 Model Predictive Control Technique

The model predictive control technique can be illustrated as shown in Fig. 2, where the controller consists of the NN SWNCS model and the optimisation block. The optimisation block determines the values of $\overline{u}$ that minimises the performance index J, and then the optimal u is input to the SWNCS. The controller block is implemented in MATLAB/Simulink, while the SWNCS block is implemented in TrueTime. The MPC method is based on the retreating horison technique. The NN model predicts the SWNCS response over a specified time horizon. The predictions are employed by a numerical optimisation plan to establish the control signal that minimises the subsequent performance index over the specified horizon (Al-Azzawi and Al-Akaidi 2012).

$$J = \frac{1}{\varepsilon_2 N}\left\{\sum_{j=1}^{\varepsilon_2}\left[t(k+j) - Y_M(k+j)\right]^2 + \partial\sum_{j=1}^{N}\left[\overline{u}(k+j-1) - \overline{u}(k+j-2)\right]^2\right\} \quad (8)$$

where N is the horizon over which the tracking error and the control increases are calculated, $\overline{u}$ is the variable provisional control signal, y_M is NN SWNCS model response, and ∂ establishes the part that the sum of the squares of control increases has on the performance index. NN predictive controllers improve tracking performance by reducing the effect of time delays on SWNCS. The basic working principle of the NN predictive controller is to generate a sequence of control signals at each sample interval that optimise the control effort in order to track exactly the desired signal. The neural-network-based predictive control signal is obtained from minimising the predictive performance index Eq. (12) over the specified horizon as follows (Al-Azzawi and Al-Akaidi 2020):

$$u(k) = [u(k)u(k+1)\ldots u(k+N)] \quad (9)$$

The control signal in (9) is found from optimisation of the performance index (8) based upon the gradient descent method, that is:

where.

Then the expression of the NNPC controller can be written in the following form

$$u(k) = u(k-1) + \lambda C^{\mathrm{T}} e(k) \quad (10)$$

where

$$C(k) = \left[\frac{\delta y_p(k)}{\delta u(k)} \frac{\delta y_p(k+1)}{\delta u(k)} \ldots \frac{\delta y_p(k+N)}{\delta u(k)}\right]^{\mathrm{T}}$$

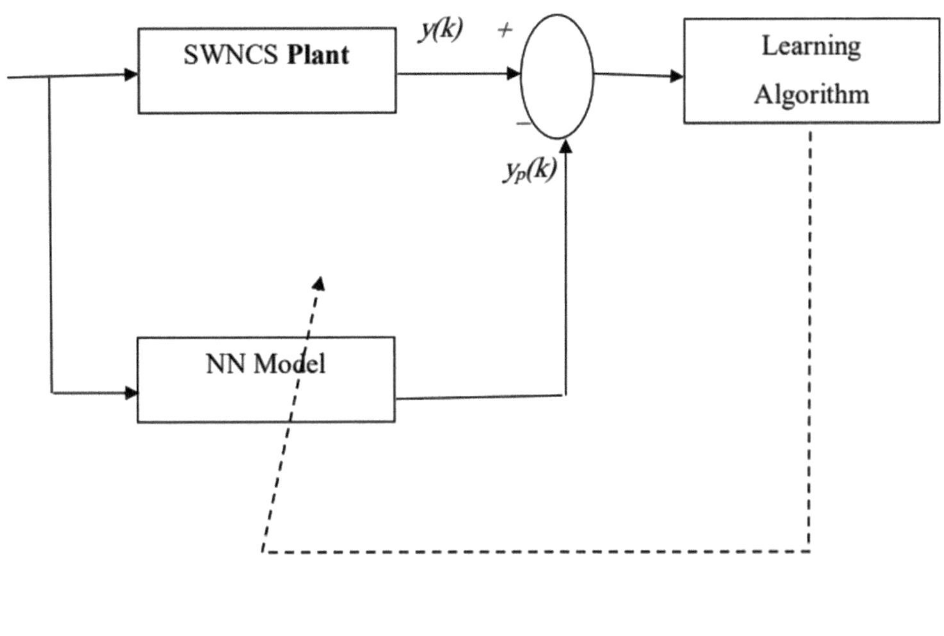

Fig. 2 System identification diagram

2.2 Stochastic Network Time Delay and Packet Dropout of SWNCS Architecture

The control signal sequence is started in the sensor, and the real time of the controller is unknown without clock synchronisation. Further, it is also not required in the proposed approach. Hence, at recent time k, the previous information of the physical plant before $k - \tau_k^{sc}$ is presented on the controller area as follows:

$$\begin{bmatrix} y_p\left(k - \tau_k^{sc}\right) \\ y_p\left(k - \tau_k^{sc} - 1\right) \\ \vdots \\ y_p\left(k - \tau_k^{sc} - N\right) \end{bmatrix}, \begin{bmatrix} u\left(k - \tau_k^{sc} - 1\right) \\ u\left(k - \tau_k^{sc} - 2\right) \\ \vdots \\ u\left(k - \tau_k^{sc} - N\right) \end{bmatrix} \tag{11}$$

Based on (10) and (11), the response predictions can be determined by the following equation:

$$\begin{cases} U(k) = \bar{\bar{U}}(k) & \text{if new information packet recived} \\ U(k) = U(k-1) & \text{otherwise} \end{cases}$$

Hence, the content of the schedule $U(k)$ is the newest control signal prediction sequence existing in the actuator node at time k, which can be expressed by:

$$U(k) = \begin{bmatrix} u\left(k - \tau_k^{sc} - \tau_k^{ca} | k - \tau_k^{sc} - \tau_k^{ca}\right) \\ u\left(k - \tau_k^{sc} - \tau_k^{ca} + 1 | k - \tau_k^{sc} - \tau_k^{ca}\right) \\ \vdots \\ u\left(k - \tau_k^{sc} - \tau_k^{ca} + N | k - \tau_k^{sc} - \tau_k^{ca}\right) \end{bmatrix} \tag{12}$$

where $k - \tau_k^{sc} - \tau_k^{ca}$ is the sampling time of the control signal predication sequence at the actuator node.

In order to remove or reduce the effect of the time delay that occurs in SWNCS, the NNPC chooses the proper control signal from (12) based on the forward and backward channel delays (i.e. τ_k^{sc} and τ_k^{ca}). Thus, the control signal input to the physical plant at time k will be

$$u(k) = u\left(k | k - \tau_k^{sc} - \tau_k^{ca}\right) \tag{13}$$

In order to validate the effectiveness of the proposed method, the following numerical example is considered, where the parameters of the discrete-time physical plant with sampling time T_s=0.01 sec are described as follows:

$$x(k+1) = \begin{bmatrix} 2.1123 & 0.0502 \\ 1.4943 & 1.0123 \end{bmatrix} X(k) + \begin{bmatrix} 0.123 \\ 0.678 \end{bmatrix} u\left(k - \tau_k^{ca}\right) + \begin{bmatrix} 0.1 \\ 0.1 \end{bmatrix} r(k)$$

$$y(k) = \begin{bmatrix} 1 & 0 \end{bmatrix} X(k)$$

The block involves SWNCS in the TrueTime model as in Fig. 3.

3 Simulation Results

The simulated NNPC for the SWNCS is illustrated in Fig. 6 with the following parameters: the cost horizon $N_2 = 7$, the control horizon $N_u = 4$, the control weighting factor $\sigma = 0.09$, search parameter $\alpha = 0.01$ and iteration per sample time = 2. When, plant identification in Fig. 4 is selected, another window appears as shown in Fig. 5. To

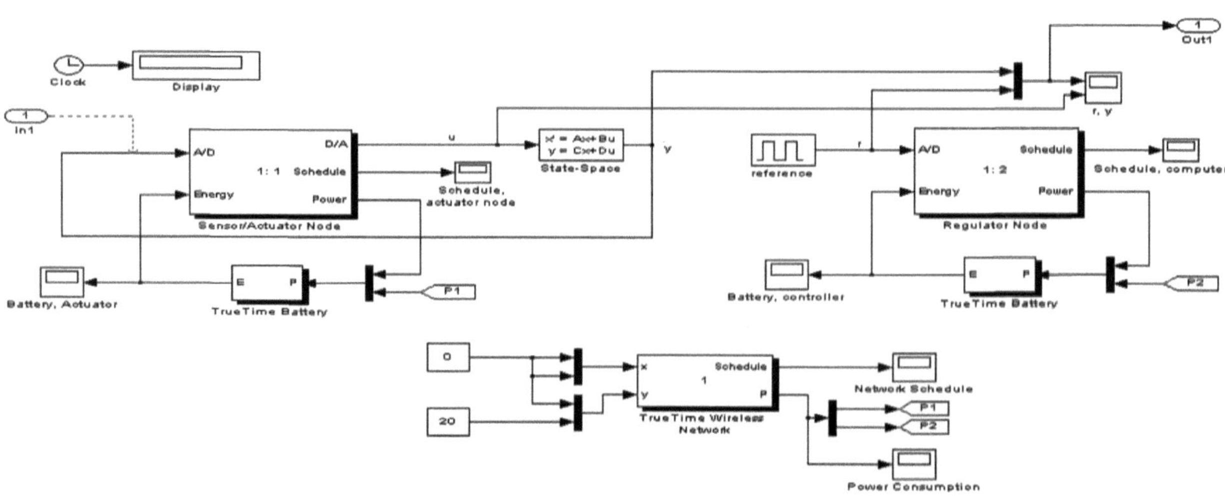

Fig. 3 SWNCS simulated in TrueTime

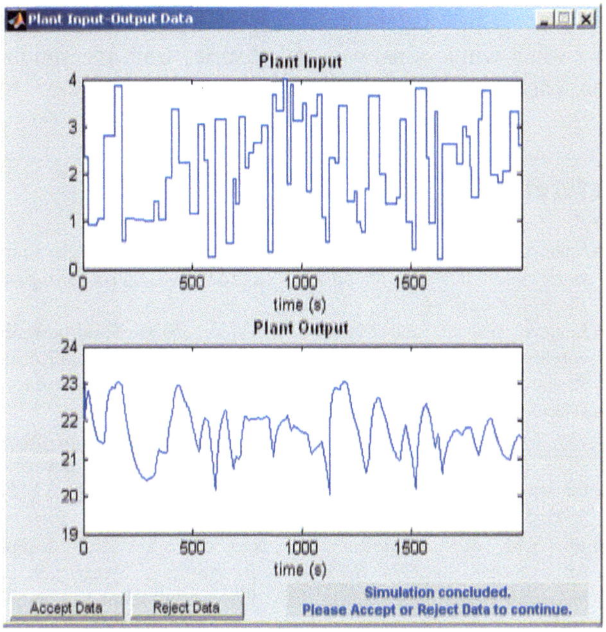

Fig. 4 Random generated SWNCS Input/output Data

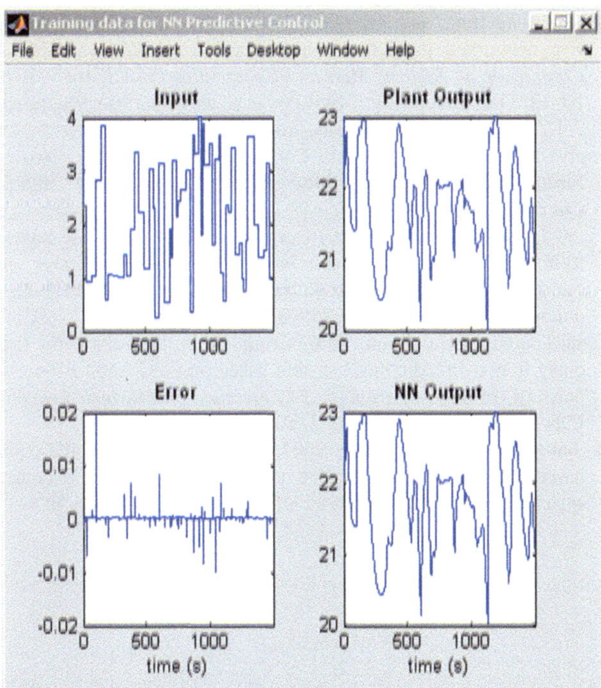

Fig. 5 Training data for SWNCS model

design NNPC, the NN SWNCS model must be developed. The SWNCS model predicts future SWNCS responses. The optimisation algorithm employs these predictions to establish the control signal that optimise future performance. In this work, the SWNCS model has an input layer, a hidden layer and an output layer. The training function described in the BP trainalgorithm is used to train the NN SWNCS model with the following parameters:

4 Network Architecture

Size of hidden layer = 5, 7 and 10, sampling interval = 0.8 s, training data. Training sample = 10,000, maximum interval value = 50 s, minimum interval value = 12 s.

Figure 5 illustrates the random training data for the SWNCS model. 10,000 training samples will be generated before training the NN SWNCS model. Select accept data, and then, select train network from plant identification window with the following training parameters (training Epochs = 500 and training function = trainlm). Figure 6 demonstrates NN training parameters such as the performance in (a) and training state in (b). The used NN training parameters like the size of hidden layer = 5, 7, 10 are presented. The SWNCS response when using the Wi-Fi as wireless network and the reference signal is shown in Fig. 7. The simulation results show that the proposed method is capable of controlling SWNCS with satisfactory tracking performance under stochastic wireless network delay (Al-Azzawi and Al-Akaidi 2020).

5 Conclusions

In this paper, the modelling schemes for SWNCSs have been analysed, and a new modelling method stimulated from the theory of variable sampling time has been introduced. In this method, the wireless network time delay was taken as the variable sampling time. The variable sampling time model was specified, where the wireless network time delay and packet dropout occurred in the system parameters. To avoid the effect of stochastic time delay existing in SWNCS, a methodology that employs NNPC to remove or reduce the effect of time delay in SWNCS and to employ the value modified by BPNN error predictive model to manage the SWNCS time delays has been presented.

The NNPC model is used to recursively calculate the output predictions and control signal predictions. To analyse the performance of the proposed scheme, a numerical simulation has been carried out. Due to the acceptable performance parameters that obtained in simulation, the simulation results have successfully illustrated the effectiveness of the proposed approach. NNPC simulations indicated that this new approach alleviated the effect of the wireless network time delay and packet dropout to the maximum extent and enhanced the performance of the control system. The

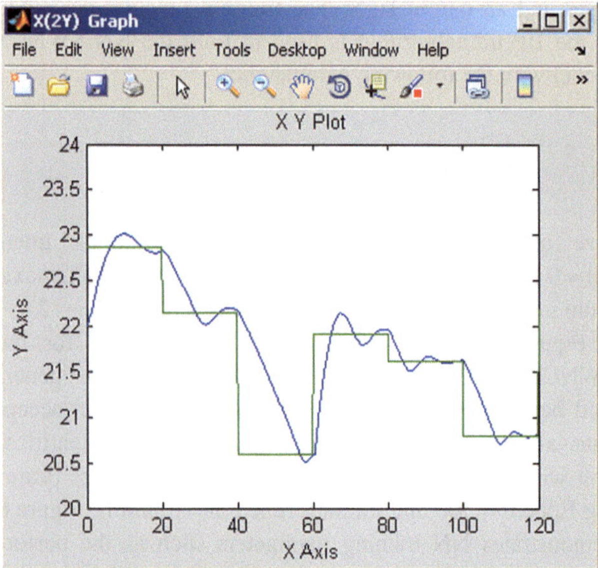

Fig. 6 SWNCS response with Wi-Fi wireless network

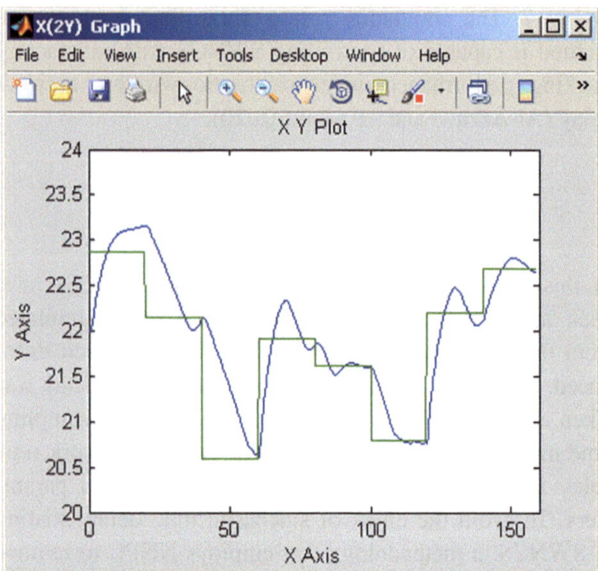

Fig. 7 Schedule at computer node

performance parameters of the proposed method are acceptable when wireless network delay varies from the simulation. The method is also rapid and adaptable.

References

Al-Azzawi, Waleed, and Marwan Al-Akaidi. 2012. Solar wireless network system based on nueral network predictive control. *European Journal of Control*.

Al-Azzawi, Waleed, and Marwan Al-Akaidi. 2020. Solar-powered wireless networked control system. Science & Engineering Research Support Society. *International Journal of Advanced Science and Technology, Acceptance*.

Elsersy, M., T.M. Elfouly, and M.H. Ahmed. 2016. Optimal placement, routing, and flow assignment in wireless sensor networks for structural health monitoring. *IEEE Sensors Journal* 16 (12): 5095–5106.

Magdi, S.M. 2014. Wireless networked control system design: An overview. In *2014 IEEE 23rd International Symposium on Industrial Electronics (ISIE)*, ISBN: 978-1-4799-2399-1, Istanbul, Turkey.

Neumann, P. 2016. Communication in industrial automation-what is going on? *Control Engineering Practice, Special Issue on Manufacturing Plant Control: Challenges and Issues INCOM 2004* 15(11): 1332–1347.

Pang, Zhong-Hua, and Guo-Ping Liu. 2010. Model-based recursive networked predictive control. In *2010 IEEE International Conference on Systems Man and Cybernetics (SMC)*, 1665–1670. 10–13 Oct 2010. http://www.doc.ic.ac.uk/nd/surpise_96/journal/vol4/CS11/report.htm#theback-propagationalgorithm.

Ploplys, N.J. 2015. *Wireless Control of Mechanical Systems. Mechanical Engineering*, MSc thesis, University of Illinois, Champaign.

Sauer, S., and W.-J. Fischer. 2016. An irreversible single-use humidity-threshold monitoring sensor principle for wireless passive sensor solutions. *IEEE Sensors Journal* 16 (18): 6920–6930. https://doi.org/10.1109/JSEN.2016.2590837.

Wang T., and Li-Hui Zhou. 2007. Complete compensation for time delay in networked control system based on GPC AND BP neural network. In *Sixth International Conference on Machine Learning Cybernetics*, Hong Kong, 19–22 Aug 2007.

Yi, Jianqiang, and Qian Wang. 2007. BP neural network prediction-based variable-period sampling approach for networked control systems. *Applied Mathematics and Computation* 185: 976–988.

Sustainability Assessment in Manufacturing from Industry 4.0 Perspective for SMEs: A Case Study in Abrasive Waterjet Machining for Hard-To-Cut Materials

Yakub Iqbal Mogul and Peter Myler

Abstract

The 4th Industrial Revolution incorporates the digital revolution in several fields, including artificial intelligence, autonomous vehicles, IoT, manufacturing, etc. Due to the advancement in difficult-to-cut materials, technology like abrasive waterjet machine (AWJM) in non-traditional manufacturing has been a benefit to the industry, and it can almost cut any material and is also considered environmentally friendly. The machine uses water, abrasives and electricity which are natural resources, and the purpose of the study is to optimize these resources for the AWJM which are relatively very complex considering the different varying parameters and material properties. The methodology is discussed with a case study of NC 3015S AWJ machine for studying sustainability using different method/tools like SCLM, ABCD and TSPDs approach which will illustrate the combined technical and sustainability assessment. An approach for working with abrasive waterjet machine on reducing cost and machining time which focusses on the four pillars of sustainability (social, economic, environmental and technology) has been presented. The discussions are demonstrated by cost/hour calculations, i.e., 45$/h for machining Ti6AL4V material, and how different machine and cutting parameters affect the total process economy was understood with abrasives contributed almost 65% of the total cost. Furthermore, a cloud-based knowledge sharing model is proposed by linking the sustainability with technology and how it can benefit the current SMEs to improve their productivity with abrasive waterjet machines.

Keywords

Sustainability · Manufacturing · Industry 4.0 · Abrasive waterjet · SMEs · Hard to cut materials · Cloud · Ti6AL4V

1 Introduction

Sustainability can be defined as the capacity to reserve, or to preserve something. The sustainability dimensions are social, economic, environment and technology can be added as the 4th parameter (Baud 2008). Sustainable process has minimum impact on the environment and which is advantageous for society and economical (Gupta et al. 2016). Sustainability is instigated by improving the processes, reduction in consumption of resources, work practices, and minimalizing the impacts through the product life cycle as in Fig. 1. To achieve sustainability, the resource consumption should be reduced. The manufacturing systems should be designed to support the unremitting waste reduction and recycling. This can be attained by collective recycling/re-usage, less generation of waste, materials, energy and efficient usage of water. Considering the current global competitiveness and strict environment regulations has forced manufacturers (SMEs) to practice industrial sustainability in manufacturing by minimizing the dependency of natural resources (TheIet.org 2020). Geographically most of the countries have started practicing industrial sustainability, many countries like UAE (UAEsdgs.ae 2020) and UK (Imeche.org. 2020; Eandt.theiet.org. 2020) have identified the key trends of automations and digitalization's and have taken industrial sustainability as a priority to reduce the impact of manufacturing on the environment by reducing waste and minimizing natural resources.

Y. I. Mogul (✉)
University of Bolton, RAK Academic Centre, P.O Box 16038, Ras al Khaimah, UAE
e-mail: y.iqbal@bolton.ac.uk

P. Myler
University of Bolton, Deane Road, Bolton BL3 5AB, UK

© The Author(s), under exclusive license to Springer Nature Switzerland AG 2024
A. Salman and A. Tharwat (eds.), *ICT for Engineering & Critical Infrastructures*, Advances in Science, Technology & Innovation, https://doi.org/10.1007/978-3-031-49309-6_2

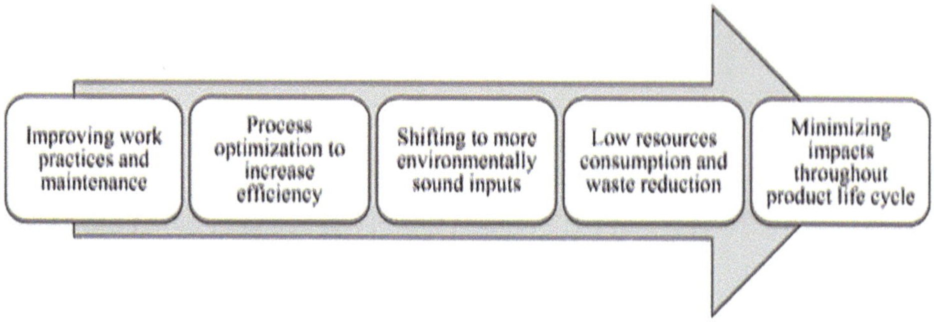

Fig. 1 Implementing sustainable manufacturing

1.1 Industry 4.0 Perspective

Sustainability and digitalization are diagonal themes covering different areas of the manufacturing chain. In fact, both methods present convergence and practices such as: remanufacturing/recycling for circular economy, "lean and green management" for resource efficiency. In general, benefits of sustainability in Industry 4.0 are anticipated on: flexibility, cultivating productivity and resource efficiency (e.g., Big Data for fast production systems and predictive maintenance); reduction on consumption of energy, waste and overproduction (e.g., surplus renewable energy shared with other plants) (Machado et al. 2020).

2 Sustainability Assessment

The different domain of sustainability can be seen in Fig. 2 with the 4th domain being the technology integrated with the 3 pillars of sustainability which can add leverage to sustainability in the manufacturing domain.

Fig. 2 Merging of sustainability with Industry 4.0 considering Technology as 4th Pillar (Baud 2008)

Table 1 summarizes the different aspects to be considered in the sustainability assessment for all the four pillars.

Table 1 Sustainability assessment

3 pillars of sustainability			4th pillar of industry 4.0
Economic	Social	Environment	Technology
Production cost includes	Noise	Recyclable waste	Artificial intelligence
Facility cost/Rent cost	Safe and healthy workplace	Recycling of water	(IoT)
Raw material cost		Energy consumption	Cybersecurity
Labor cost		Gaseous waste	Big Data Analytics
			Additive manufacturing

3 Case Study: Abrasive Waterjet Cutting Machine (NC3015S)

3.1 Relevance of the Case Study

Case study on abrasive waterjet cutting (AWJC) is discussed in this section, which is a current and sustainable manufacturing technology. Its advantage includes high flexibility and accuracy, minimum losses in work piece material and copious main processing substances, i.e., sand (Abrasives) and water. It can cut different types of hard to cut material with varying thicknesses and low thermal (no HAZ) and mechanical influence on the work piece. The study material in this case study was titanium alloy, Ti6AL4V, and slot cutting was done to understand the cut quality and depth of cut with Taguchi-DoE (Design of Experiments) methods.

3.2 Abrasive Waterjet Cutting (AWJC) Technology

AWJC is a manufacturing technique which uses sand (Abrasives) and water to shape the workpiece with an erosion process. High-pressurized water with a mix of abrasives passes through a slender nozzle within the cutting head; a high amount of energy is concentrated in a small area and thereby creating the power for cutting. Abrasive waterjet cutting machine which is considered in the case study is illustrated in Fig. 3. NC3015S is an abrasive water jet machine which is manufactured by Water jet Sweden AB. Water jet Sweden is an ISO 9001:2000 certified company. The machine specifications are provided in Table 2.

3.3 Case Study Sustainability Assessment Procedure

Initial step in assessment for sustainability is to have an initial understanding of the machinery and its working conditions. Here, the emphasis is on abrasive water jet cutting machine—in current condition as well in a sustainable future. The focused is around technical performance like quality of cut/depth of cut and the time taken for the slot cutting in the material. The assessments for sustainability were carried out using various tools/methods like:

- *Listing the Sustainability benefits/problems and action ideas follow-on from TSPDs* (Table 3)

TSPD is a method to interconnect and compile descriptive statements from an expert within sustainability domain on

Fig. 3 NC 3015S abrasive waterjet machine

Table 2 Specification for water jet NC 3015 S

Specification for water jet NC 3015 S	
• Software: IGEMS	• Pressure: 0–4200 Bar
• Motion System: Ball screw (X &Y)	• Pump: KMT (SLIV Plus) 50hp
• Control System: Fanuc CNC	• Flow rate: 0–3.6 L/min
• Cutting Bed Dimension (Width × length): 3200 mm × 1750 mm	• Abrasive: Garnet
• X. Y and Z movement = 3010, 1510, 250 mm	

Table 3 Sustainability benefits/problems/ideas follow-on from TSPDs (Byggeth et al. 2007)

TSPDs for Water Jet Cutting for Hard-to-Cut Materials			
B (Current problems/Benefits)	**I. Market Needs/Desires**	**II. Perceptions**	**III. Extended Initiative**
	Present market needs addressed:	**Theoretical design of today's product:**	**Current communiqué/cooperation:**
	"Water jet is used to cut different hard to cut materials and composites with high accuracy in applications like aircraft and automobile industries"	"Water jet cutting uses natural resources like water, abrasives and thereby contributes to increasing natural wastages"	"There is a lack of understanding in recycling of abrasives/water management and electricity consumption"
	"Waterjet is a resource efficient and relatively safe cutting technology with no damage to the workpiece (no HAZ)"	"In built sophisticated software's to take decision on different parameter's to be used for the process"	"Knowledge of optimized parameters for different cutting application for specific materials"
C (Future Action Ideas)	**Future market requirements to address**	**Theoretical design of future product:**	**Future communiqué/cooperation:**
	"Cutting speed and accuracy will need to be improved"	"Decision making of the parameters provided for the cutting"	"Robust software's well connected with databases for decision making"
	"Recycling of water, abrasives and usage of electricity"	"Focus on a self sufficient system with internal recycling of sand and water and minimum usage of electricity"	"Start strategic cooperation with material recycling and electricity usage"

probable sustainability benefits/problems of a considered idea and possible related solutions (Ny et al. 2008). This is to generate imagination in teams and initiate their sustainability assessment from a knowledgeable platform. In this study, the template method was used for the predominant sustainability benefits/problems and principle solutions for the water jet cutting company.

- *ABCD and SLCM assessment for Sustainability Principle* (Table 4)
- *SLCM assessment for ABCD steps. How action ideas are prioritized and planned* (Table 5)

ABCD and SLCM are tools/approaches for predominant sustainability assessments. An ABCD recognizes the important possible sustainability-related complications and principle solutions for an activity/product. The assessment can be elevated to an SLCM by more steadily infusing it into a life-cycle overview, including manufacturing, reuse/use, disposal or recycling. Both approaches also give recommendations for how to rank between probable solutions to the issues. The study uses SLCM and makes an initial predominant actioned plan for the waterjet cutting and its life cycle activities.

- *Cost and Time analysis.*

4 Cost Analysis for Cutting Titanium Grade 5 Alloy (Ti6AL4V) with NC 3015 S Abrasive Waterjet Machine

The categories considered for the calculation of cost of waterjet cutting:

(1) **Operating cost**—Operating cost is associated with many factors; it includes consumption of electrical energy, water consumption, abrasive consumption

Table 4 B and C steps from an SLCM assessment

ABCD assessment setup	Parameters		Life cycle phases	Waste management
B (Current problems/ benefits)				
SP1	Knowledge of parameters used for the reduction of resources	Consumption of Electricity for operating pump/Machines		Consumption of fuels in transporting water removals
SP2	....	...		....
SP3	....	...		....
C (Action Concepts)	Design for recycling and optimize parameters for various materials	– Design improvement for material loss and consumption of energy – Jet efficiency Improvement – understanding material lifecycle and use of energy		Smart machining would reduce waste elimination and resource transportation
	-......	-...		-...

Sustainability benefits/problems (B-step) and ideas (C-step) (Byggeth et al. 2007)

Table 5 Ideas (C-step) and Step D of an SLCM assessment (Byggeth et al. 2007)

Actions to be taken	Importance/Time slots		
	Very high (Year 1)	High (Year 2–5)	Medium to low (Year 6+)
– Energy/material lifecycle understanding	//////////////		
– Energy/material reduction through improvement in system design	//////////////		
– Designing for recycling/reuse	/////////////////////////////////		
– Efficiency in jet	/////////////////////////////////		
– Improvement in knowledge-based optimized parameters for the cutting	///		

is the maximum of all, parts wear, repair and maintenance. These costs are basically considered during the machine operating time.

(2) **Labour cost**—It is associated with the duration of machine running; it includes time for raw material handling, finished parts. To include a costs, the operator hourly cost, the time it takes to make a part on machine, the machine setup time, and the time an operator attends the machine should be known. These parameters all may be different for each machine or facility.

(3) **Maintenance** and other cost associated with the machine.

4.1 Influencing Parameters for Abrasive Waterjet Cutting and Its Cost

The process of cutting in abrasive waterjet machine depends on many process parameters, which include pump pressure, nozzle/orifice diameter, cutting speed, abrasive mass flow rate, etc., and all these parameters had a pronounced effect on the speed of cut, quality of parts and cost of the part. Water pump is the most important part in determining the operating costs for the waterjet. Water pressure has a high influence in the parts cut quality. Abrasive constitutes around more than 60% of the machine operating cost.

Table 6 shows the parameters considered to cut the titanium material for the case study purpose. The pump used in the machine was 50 HP/37 kW rating; unfortunately the machine has single cutting head for all the operations, and the abrasives used were garnet for the cutting process as changing the abrasives results in an increase in the cost for the production.

4.2 Determination of Hourly Cost to Run a Waterjet Machine

As per the case study Workpiece Material: Titanium Alloy Grade 5 (Ti6AL4V), 15 mm thickness was considered with single cutting head, 50 HP/37 kW pump for NC3015S abrasive waterjet machine, and various elements are considered to understand the average cost of cutting for the considered material (Fig. 4).

From Table 7, we can observe that the abrasive contribution cost seems to be high in the cutting operation for the abrasive waterjet, apart from that spare parts and electricity cost follow the cost series, and regarding the sustainability aspects, it becomes imperative for the SMEs to think of alternative arrangements for recycling of abrasives as well knowledge of cutting parts for hard-to-cut material should be increased.

Table 6 Design of experiment parameters and levels (Mogul et al. 2020)

Symbol	AWJ cutting parameters	Level 1	Level 2	Level 3
W_p	Water pressure (bar)	2400	2900	3400
T_s	Transverse speed (mm/min)	80	100	150
A_{mf}	Abrasive mass flow rate (kg/min)	0.160	0.180	0.215
N/O_{dr}	Nozzle diameter (mm) Orifice diameter (mm)	1.2 0.25	0.77 0.35	1.0 0.30

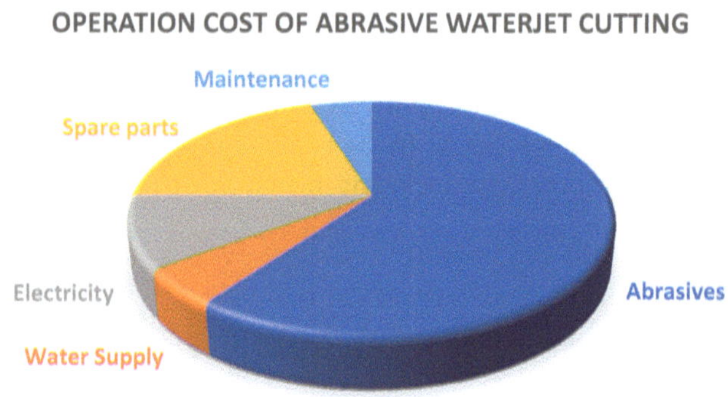

Fig. 4 Chart demonstrating various areas of operating cost of abrasive waterjet cutting

5 Sustainability Solutions to Reduce Cost for Abrasive Waterjet Cutting

Numerous ways can be introduced in order to reduce the cost of cutting in abrasive waterjet cutting, one alternative way is to think of abrasive recycle waste management systems, and more effort can be taken in terms of educating the operator community on the material cutting technology by sharing the cutting data through online mode so that the community is aware of the research which is happening in cutting various hard-to-cut materials rather being in isolation.

5.1 Recycling of Abrasive Material

Managing and reusing abrasives is good for operators, the planet. A study conducted by Hypertherm company reveals that 55% of the abrasives counts for the cost of cutting in abrasive waterjet. A Canadian company Known as Fabricating and Welding developed a abrasive recycling waste management system in which they were able to recycle the abrasive at least three times and cut down the cost,

Table 7 Cost/hour calculation for cutting with abrasive waterjet cutting (Radovanovic 2007)

Abrasive waterjet cutting machine, Single head, 50 HP/37 kW			
Workpiece material: titanium alloy grade 5 (Ti6AL4V), 15 mm thickness			
Item	Cost	Longevity	Cost/ Hour
Ruby orifice	$17	40 h	0.42$/h
Nozzle	$80	80 h	1$/h
Low-pressure seals	$90	9000 h	0.01$/h
High-pressure seals	$100	1000 h	0.1$/h
Power (50 HP Pump)	$0.122 kWh	–	$4.88/h
Cutting water (50 Hp, 4 gpm)	4.0 gpm	–	$0.35/h
Cooling water (50Hp, 1 gpm)	10 gpm	–	$0.95/h
Electricity power consumption	37 kW	–	–
Electrical energy unit cost	0.10$/kWh	–	–
Total electrical energy cost	–	–	3.7$/h
Unit cost of water consumption	0.13$/IG	–	–
Water consumption	4.0 gpm	–	–
Cost of water	–	–	0.12$/h
Sewerage	–	–	0.014$/ unit
Abrasive consumption	35 kg/h	–	–
Unit cost of abrasive	–	–	0.78$/kg
Cost of abrasives	–	–	27.3$/h
Wear cost of orifice	–	–	0.067$/h
Wear cost of nozzle	–	–	0.67$/h
Maintenance cost		–	1.40$/h
Labour cost	820$/month	–	3.40$/h
Waterjet cost/h	**–**	**–**	**45$/h**

Note The above costs are the averaged cost assumed at the duration, the costs may vary subject to different countries and government policies, and also the costs do not include the material cost, investment cost and the depreciation cost of the machine

and total recovery rate of the abrasive after the 3 phases is between 45.5 and 78.5%, but this system can only be used where the SMEs used garnet in a very large quantity on a daily and the investment money can be recovered after 2 years of installation period.

Dong et al. (2014) developed an approach for online abrasives recycling by utilizing a stirring overflow separator to understand the separation of abrasives and dirt. Due to the impact in cleaning process, abrasives are broken into pieces, and it makes the process more sustainable, greener and economical by recycling the abrasives in abrasives waterjet machining.

5.2 Cloud-Based Knowledge Data Sharing Model for Abrasive Water Jet Machining

All the abrasive waterjet machines have their standalone software which can help in improving the cutting process, but there is a lack of knowledge within the manufacturing domain about the optimized parameters to be used for hard-to-cut materials, and because of this, SMEs are not able to share their knowledge in this domain. For example for control depth milling, very less research is available as there is a wider gap in the SMEs to obtain the optimal parameters for a material to perform the task, and the proposed model can help the current waterjet industry to share the research data through a web-based cloud platform and at the other end through a web portal the operator can access the research and understanding about the parameters undertaken to carry out a task as per the requirements (Fig. 5).

6 Conclusion

Technology has become the most important pillar in relation to Industry 4.0 for the current era; the current manufacturing units should become smart so that they can exchange knowledge and ideas related to the optimization of their process in order to reduce the waste generated and recycling of the resources available. Also, efforts can be made to tackle the situation at the design level of the machinery. The cutting cost of the material can be further reduced with the in-depth knowledge of all the areas of manufacturing.

7 Future Recommendations

An in-depth study should be carried out how the abrasive waterjet machine can be made a "smart manufacturing machine" with exchange of ideas and knowledge through web based application, more knowledge can be generated for the different composite materials which are still difficult to cut with the abrasive waterjet machine.

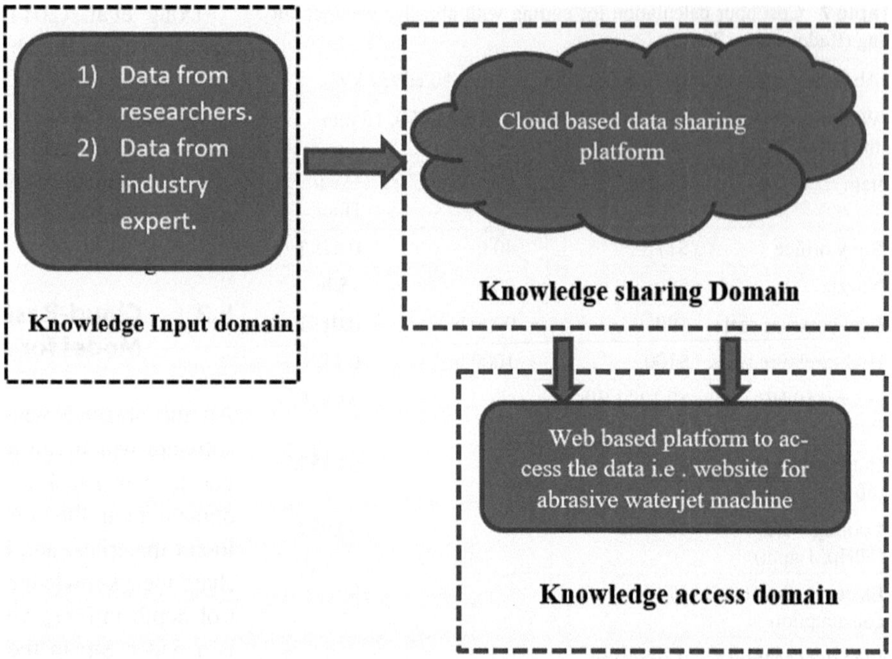

Fig. 5 Proposed cloud-based knowledge data sharing model for abrasive water jet machining

References

Andersson, U., and G. Holmqvist. 2005. Strategies for cost—and time-effective use of abrasive waterjet cutting. In *WJTA American Waterjet Conference*, 7B-2. Houston, Texas.

Baud, R.2008. The concept of sustainable development: Aspects and their consequences from a social-philosophical perspective. In *YES Youth Encounter on Sustainability Summer Course Material*, 8–27.

Byggeth Sophie, H., N. Henrik, W. Johan, B. Göran, and R. Karl-Henrik. 2007. Introductory procedure for sustainability-driven design optimization. In *Guidelines for a Decision Support Method Adapted to NPD Processes*.

Dong, Y., W. Liu, H. Zhang, and H. Zhang. 2014. On-line recycling of abrasives in abrasive water jet cleaning. *Procedia Cirp* 15: 278–282.

Eandt.theiet.org. 2020. Sustainable manufacturing: The industrial ecosystem. Available at: https://eandt.theiet.org/content/articles/2010/08/sustainable-manufacturing-the-industrial-ecosystem/. Accessed 31 Jan 2020.

Gupta, K., R.F. Laubscher, J.P. Davim, and N.K. Jain. 2016. Recent developments in sustainable manufacturing of gears: A review. *Journal of Cleaner Production* 112: 3320–3330.

Imeche.org. 2020. Professional engineering and sage report shows manufacturing split on 2020 growth prospects. Available at: https://www.imeche.org/news/news-article/professional-engineering-and-sage-report-shows-manufacturing-split-on-2020-growth-prospects. Accessed 31 Jan 2020.

Kmtwaterjet.com. 2020. Available at: https://www.kmtwaterjet.com/KMT%20Streamline%20SL-V%20Pumps%20Catalog.pdf. Accessed 21 June 2020.

Mogul, Y.I., I. Nasir, and P. Myler. 2020. Investigation and optimization for depth of cut and surface roughness for control depth milling in Titanium Ti6AL4V with abrasive water jet cutting. *Materials Today: Proceedings*.

Ny, H., S. Hallstedt, K.H. Robèrt, and G. Broman. 2008. Introducing templates for sustainable product development: A case study of televisions at the Matsushita Electric Group. *Journal of Industrial Ecology* 12 (4): 600–623.

Oztemel, E. and S. Gursev 2020. Literature review of Industry 4.0 and related technologies. *Journal of Intelligent Manufacturing* 31(1): 127–182.

Pegas Engineering. 2020. Water Jet Sweden AB. Available at: http://pegas-engineering.pl/en/machine-park/water-jet-sweden-ab/. Accessed 21 June 2020.

Radovanovic, M. 2007. Abrasive waterjet cutting cost. *Nonconventional Technologies Review* 1: 97–102.

Radovanović, Miroslav. 2020. Abrasive waterjet cutting cost.

Sartal, A., R. Bellas, A.M. Mejías, and A. García-Collado. 2020. The sustainable manufacturing concept, evolution and opportunities within Industry 4.0: A literature review. *Advances in Mechanical Engineering* 12(5): 1687814020925232.

Theiet.org. 2020. Why doing more with less won't cost the earth—it'll save it. Available at: https://www.theiet.org/impact-society/sectors/design-and-manufacturing/manufacturing-matters/why-doing-more-with-less-won-t-cost-the-earth-it-ll-save-it/. Accessed 31 Jan 2020

Uaesdgs.ae. 2020. The UAE portal for the sustainable development goals. Available at: https://uaesdgs.ae/en/goals/industry-innovation-and-infrastructure. Accessed 31 Jan 2020.

WARDJet. 2020. Hourly cost to run a waterjet. Available at: https://wardjet.com/waterjet/cost-to-run-a-waterjet. Accessed 21 June 2020.

Welding, C. 2020. Cut waterjet cutting cost. Canadianmetalworking.com. Available at: https://www.canadianmetalworking.com/canadianfabricatingandwelding/article/fabricating/cut-waterjet-cutting-cost. Accessed 21 June 2020.

Zhang, H., and K.R. Haapala. 2012 Integrating sustainability assessment into manufacturing decision making. In *Leveraging Technology for a Sustainable World*, 551–556. Berlin: Springer.

Dual Shock: Impact of COVID-19 and Fall in Oil Prices from GCC Perspective

Sania Ashraf

Abstract

The study examines the effect of COVID-19, plunge in oil prices and stock market returns of Gulf Council Co-operation. As the demand and supply shock of oil has disrupted the global economy with the impact of COVID-19, our study attempts to trace out the relationship existence between these variables. To investigate the effect of this pandemic and the drop in oil prices and stock returns, the study employed a panel regression approach using two measurements: (1) daily growth in total confirmed cases and (2) daily growth in total deaths caused by COVID-19. There is no research available analyzing the relationship between COVID-19, oil price fluctuations and stock market index of GCC. It is this gap that the current study tries to fill by examining the effect of COVID-19, the fall of oil prices and stock market returns of GCC. The study found that there was bi-directional causality relationship between death cases as well as confirmed cases of COVID-19 to stock market returns, also it was also found that there was a unidirectional relationship of confirmed cases of COVID-19 and oil prices in world market, leading to an effect on the stock market returns, which shows that increased confirmed cases resulted to the reduced oil prices in world market affecting the investments in the stock market.

Keywords

COVID-19 · Pandemic · Stock returns · Panel data · Oil prices · Market performance

JEL Classification

C23 · G15 · H12

1 Introduction

Stock market indices are judged as a good indicator of economic growth, firm's historical and future growth and the business climate in general. The performance of these indices is closely related to events of noneconomic nature as well. With the ongoing outbreak of COVID-19, evidently the connection between pandemics and stock market performance is under scrutiny. Though exogenous in nature, pandemics or infectious diseases have left both short-term and long-term effects on economic performance of countries affected. Historically, the worst pandemic occurred at the beginning of the twentieth century with the outbreak of Spanish flu in 1918, which killed more than 50 million people and infected more than 500 million worldwide. Since then, the world has faced many other outbreaks of pandemic nature such as Asian Flu, Hong Kong Flu, HIV, SARS, Swine Flu, MERS, Ebola and the latest being COVID-19.

Most economists and financial experts are of the opinion that the current COVID-19 outbreak closely resembles the Great Influenza pandemic in terms of its economic impact. Barro and Ursúa (2008) estimated that this pandemic can be ranked as the fourth most important global macroeconomic shock, the others being the two World Wars and the Great Depression of the early 1930s. They estimated that the Great Influenza Pandemic shrank the real per capita GDP if a typical economy by 6% and consumption by 8.1%.

A large section of experts compared the financial effects of COVID-19 to that of the Great Recession (GR) of 2008 which was otherwise referred to as Great Financial Crisis (GFC). However, Harvey (2020) referred to the current crisis as the 'Great Compression' and pointed out that the structural problems of the US economy catalyzed and

S. Ashraf (✉)
Dubai Business School, University of Dubai, Dubai, UAE
e-mail: saniaashrafpp1@gmail.com

© The Author(s), under exclusive license to Springer Nature Switzerland AG 2024

A. Salman and A. Tharwat (eds.), *ICT for Engineering & Critical Infrastructures*,
Advances in Science, Technology & Innovation, https://doi.org/10.1007/978-3-031-49309-6_3

aggravated the financial crisis of 2008. He pointed out that the current crisis is more of a systemic risk, with equal impact across countries, which makes it different from the Great Recession. Affected by anxiety, people rate the future returns down and tend to take fewer risk (Kaplanski and Levy 2010). The market response to extreme incidents such as environment disasters, pandemics or political events has generally been pessimistic, and it leads to a downfall of stock indices and return on assets in general. This observation proved true about the current COVID-19 pandemic as well. Herd reaction or low institutional participation could make the downfall of the indices more pronounced (Donadelli et al. 2016; Zouaoui et al. 2011).

As COVID-19 spread through various parts of the world, the Chinese stock markets registered the biggest single day loss as indicated by the Shanghai and Shenzhen composite indices recorded on January 23, 2020. Similarly, the volatility of the US stock markets reflected the effect of 'bad sentiments' emerging from the COVID-19 outbreak in the 22 trading days from February 24 to March 24, 2020. During the same period, the US policy uncertainty added to the loss of more than one-third of the global capital (Chinanews.com 2020; Baker et al. 2020). Similar to the trend in the US markets, the Middle East stock markets also rallied in response to the pandemic. On March 1, 2020, it was reported that the Dubai Financial Market dipped 4.3%, while the Abu Dhabi market recorded 3.8% fall. Qatar Stock Exchange Index dropped 0.6%, Bahrain Stock Market recorded a loss of 2.1%, and Muscat Securities Market in Oman lost 0.6%. To make matters worse, there was a concurrent decrease in crude oil price due to concerns over global demand which was amplified by the price war between Russia and Saudi Arabia (Arabian News.com 2020).

In this context, this paper tries to analyze the impact of COVID-19 and the oil price slump on the stock market index of GCC. In our effort to make the relationship between these variables clear, we discuss the available literature in the next part. Section 2 provides a literature review; Sect. 3 describes the dataset and the empirical methodology; Sect. 4 presents an analysis of the empirical results; and Sect. 5 concludes and provides some policy implications.

2 Review of Literature

It was on December 31, 2019, that the Chinese government informed the World Health Organization (WHO) about the occurrence of a disease with symptoms similar to Flu in patients in Wuhan, Hubei province. By January 21, 2020, over 100,000 persons around the world were infected. While the fear of the disease growing to pandemic proportions, the financial markets reported downfall based on pessimistic sentiments. Anticipating the decrease in demand for crude oil Saudi Arabia started a price war on March 9, 2020, flooding the market with excess supply. This led the sharpest fall oil prices and stock indices world over since the Spanish Flu pandemic called the Black Monday. Table 1 presented represents the drop in the major stock market indices until March 15, 2020.

The economies of the Middle East being strongly dependent on the oil exploration and extraction were in for a shock as the COVID-19 spreads across them the highest spread being in Saudi Arabia. COVID-19 has made the economic conditions in the Middle Eastern states weaken as most of them were already affected by a reduction in trade, disruption in domestic and external demand and fall in business and investor confidence (oecd.org 2020). As on March 15, 2020, the major stock markets of Middle East such as Saudi Arabia, Abu Dhabi, Dubai, Egypt, Bahrain and Kuwait recorded drop of nearly 10% of their specific indices, while Qatar and Oman recorded upward trend of less than 1%. The study also showed a major drop of nearly 39.24% in the price of Brent crude oil (Alam 2020).

There are several lines of argument in explaining the relationship between stock prices and oil prices. One of them postulates that with the financialization of commodity markets, oil price risk acts as a systematic risk proxy capturing global growth concerns and hence stock prices and oil prices are highly correlated (Balcilar et al. 2019). Some works in this line propose that there exists a bidirectional relationship between the two variables (Basher and Sadorsky 2016; Das et al. 2018). The second line of argument puts forth that the oil prices influence the forecast of macro-economic variables and hence Economic Policy Uncertainty (EPU) (Antonakakis et al. 2013; Kang et al. 2017). At the same time, policy uncertainty influences oil prices (Aloui et al. 2016; Yang 2019).

Exploring the relationship between the spread of COVID-19, oil price volatility and the stock market fluctuation in the USA, it was observed that the impact has to

Table 1 Drop in stock market indices

Stock index	Percentage drop for one month ending on March 16, 2020
USA Dow Jones	27.95
UK FTSE	29.72
Germany DAX	33.37
France CAX	33.63
Japan Nikkei	26.85
India Sensex	17.74
Crude Brent	39.24

Nathan (2020)

be analyzed in both the short-run and long-run perspectives. Using wavelet analysis, the researchers explored the sensitivity of the US stock market to the combined effect of COVID-19 and oil price volatility (Arshiyan et al. 2020). Another study which observed the stock returns across all companies listed in Hang Seng Index and Shanghai Stock Exchange identified that daily growth of confirmed COVID-19 cases and mortality reported, both negatively influenced the stock returns and large capitalization companies, were more negatively affected (Al-Awadhi et al. 2020).

There is very little research available analyzing the relationship between COVID-19, oil price fluctuations and stock market index of GCC. It is this gap that the current study tries to fill by examining the effect of COVID-19 on oil prices and stock market returns of GCC. As the demand and supply shock of oil has disrupted the global economy with the impact of COVID-19, our study attempts to trace out any relationship existence between these variables. We considered oil prices, stock returns, COVID-19 confirmed cases and death cases of GCC countries. To investigate the effect of this pandemic on oil prices and stock returns, we employ a panel regression approach using two measurements: (1) daily growth in total confirmed cases and (2) daily growth in total deaths caused by COVID-19.

3 Empirical Methodology

The main objective of this present research work is to examine the impact of COVID-19 and drop in oil prices on stock market returns among Gulf Council Co-operation. We considered oil prices, stock returns, COVID-19 confirmed cases and death cases of GCC countries for a period stating from March 2020 till July 2020. To investigate the effect of this pandemic on oil prices and stock returns, the study employs a panel regression approach using two measurements: (1) daily growth in total confirmed cases and (2) daily growth in total deaths caused by COVID-19. The variables used in this study are oil prices (OP), novel coronavirus confirmed cases (CC), death cases of novel coronavirus (CD) and stock market returns (SR) among Gulf countries such as UAE, Kuwait, Saudi Arabia, Oman, Bahrain and Qatar. Since the nature of the data is based on both time series and cross section, the sophisticated panel econometric models such as unit root test, co-integration test, and granger causality tests were employed to examine the impact of COVID-19 and oil prices shock on stock market returns in natural logarithm form for eliminating the heteroscedasticity of the data. The methodologies used were as follows.

3.1 Panel Unit Root Test

In econometric models, it is necessary to check the independences of the data series because it should not be dependent with the any series. For tracing out the dependence or stationarity process, the study used unit root test for the series. The following equation shows the unit root process.

$$y_{it} = \rho y_{it-1} + \delta_0 + \delta_1 t + n_i + v_t + \varepsilon_{it} \tag{1}$$

From the model testing the coefficient of ρ is equal to one, where $i = 1, 2, \ldots, N$ represent the N individual items included in the panel. Since the data is both time series and cross section, the panel unit root tests of LLC (Levin et al. 2012) and IPS (Im et al. 2003) are used to measure the independence of the series. The null hypothesis of these statistics is nonstationarity.

3.2 Panel Co-Integration Test

Co-integration test *tries* to measure the relationship between stock market returns and COVID–19 along with oil prices of these countries with respect to short-term and long-term effect. The study used famous Petroni (1999) co-integration test to find the long-term relationship between the variables. This test takes the null hypothesis of no co-integration exists between the variables. This test takes the following equation

$$S_{it} = \alpha_t + \delta_i t + \beta_{1i} X_{1it} + \ldots \beta_{mi} X_{mit} + \varepsilon_{it} \tag{2}$$

where $t = 1$, $i = 1 \ldots N$. Petroni (1999) test has seven statistics in which first test takes nonparametric variance ratio, and second and third tests take nonparametric analogues. Fourth test takes ADF corresponds. These four statistics making analysis on the base of within dimension. Rest three statistics based on group mean approach such as G-rho, G-ADF and G-PP. If any four statistics shows significance, then it can be said that there is a long-term relationship between the variables.

3.3 Panel Granger Causality Test

After investigating the short- and long-run relationship, it is necessary to find out the causality test to identify the cause and effect. The present study we used panel granger causality test based on Granger's (1969) concept. Granger causality tests measure the causal relationship with bivariate datasets, and these relationships can be expressed as unidirectional or bidirectional. Through this test, one can understand the exact variable causing with dependent variable which was used in this study. Granger causality tests used the following form:

$$Z_{it} = \sum_{j=1}^{p} \Gamma_{ijt} Z_{i,t-j} + \mu_{it} + \varepsilon_{it}, i = 1, ..., N\&t = 1, ...T \quad (3)$$

with Z_{it} K-dimensional. For the bivariate models $K=2$ with Z_{it}=[Port Performance it Port Traffic it] with '*L*' indicating natural logarithms. The vector μ_{it} contains individual specific, i.e., major ports in India and period fixed effects; $\mu_{it} = \alpha_t + \beta_t$, accounting for both common shocks and general growth difference between ports. Accordingly, we allow for at most period effects. The disturbances ε_{it} are assumed to be independently distributed across individuals and time, with means 0 and variances α_i^2, permitting individual heteroscedasticity. The parameter matrices Γ_{ijt} potentially vary with *I*, *j* and *t*. As all coefficients cannot differ, we allow for temporal heterogeneity in causal links that are assumed homogeneous across individuals, and the converse case of individual specific causal links that are invariant over time. A specific element of Γ_{ijt} is denoted by $\gamma_{ab,ijt,}$ which are of interest in granger noncausality using Wald statistic, whereas we test $H_0 : \gamma_{21,ijt,} = 0\Phi i, j, t$ to determine whether stock market returns is granger noncausal for COVID-19.

4 Results and Discussion

The results of Pooled Ordinary Least Square regression test are presented in Table 2. While using the assumption that all coefficients are constant across time and individuals, it is assumed that there is neither significant individual nor significant temporal effects, and all the data were pooled and an ordinary least squares (OLS) regression model was employed. The panel consists of data for the gulf countries, during March 2020 to July 2020. The pooled ordinary least square panel regression takes the following form;

$$SR_{it} = \propto 0 + \beta 1OP_{it} + \beta 2CC_{it} + \beta 3CD_{it} \quad (4)$$

where *i* stands for *i*th individual unit (cross-section) and t stands for *t*th time period. OP stands for oil price, CC stands for confirmed cases of corona, and CD stands for death cases of coronavirus. The robustness of parameter coefficient is used to explain the relationship between stock market returns and COVID-19. From the table, it can be interpreted that oil prices and confirmed cases of corona have positive impact on stock market returns, and death cases of corona were found to have a strong negative impact on the stock market returns of GCC. The outcome of the model shows that 1% increase in oil price leads to a rise in the growth of stock market returns by 0.22%. Similarly, 1% change in the growth of confirmed cases leads to change 0.35% to the stock market returns. The table also found that 1% change in the death cases of COVID-19 leads to change in the growth of stock market returns by 0.11%.

Table 3 presents the results of unit root test for LLC, Breitung and IPS. From the table, it can be evidenced that all the variables are accepted at the unit root hypothesis of process or nonstationarity at levels. But these variables are stationary at first difference at different confidence levels. From the results of unit root test, it can be concluded that the series are nonstationary and integrated at order one, i.e., *I* (1). At this stage, we applied co-integration test to investigate the long-run relationship, if exists, between the variables during the study period.

Table 4 presents the co-integration test which tries to measure the relationship between stock market returns and COVID-19 in both long-run and short-run effect. The present study used renowned Petroni (1999) co-integration test, which takes seven statistics to measure the relationship among the stock market returns and COVID-19. From Table 4, it can be proved that 6 out of 7 co-integration statistics shows significant results stating that there exists a long-run relationship between the variables under study.

Table 2 Relationship between stock market returns and COVID-19

Relationship between stock market returns and COVID-19
(A panel data approach)
Dependent variable: stock market returns

Explanatory variable	Co-efficient	Std error	*T*-statistic	*p*-value
Cons	−0.0014	0.0022	−0.6237	0.5344
OP	0.2250	0.0106	2.1188	0.0350**
CC	0.3550	0.0226	1.5720	0.011***
CD	−0.1100	0.0008	−0.2124	0.000***
Prob>*F*	0.0686 (2.3957)			

Table 3 Results of the panel unit root tests

Variables	LLC		Breitung		IPS	
	I(0)	*I*(1)	*I*(0)	*I*(1)	*I*(0)	*I*(1)
SR	− 1.848	− 7.705***	− 1.585	− 6.870***	0.071	0.185***
OP	− 3.052	− 6.508***	− 2.700	− 6.566***	0.157	0.108***
CC	− 1.864	− 3.694***	− 1.742	− 3.675***	0.077	0.162***
CD	8.324	− 5.423***	− 2.331	− 2.353**	0.077	0.063***

Table 4 Results of the Petroni panel co-integration tests

	Co-eff value	*p*-value
Within—dimension		
Panel v—stat	− 1.4615	0.9672
Panel rho—stat	− 7.6795***	0.0000
Panel PP—stat	− 8.4574***	0.0000
Panel ADF—stat	− 4.3262***	0.0001
Between—dimension		
Group rho—stat	− 3.9723***	0.0000
Group PP—stat	− 6.0292***	0.0000
Group ADF—stat	− 3.2114***	0.0007

Table 5 Results of the cross-country effect of COVID-19 and stock market returns

Country	OP	CC	CD	ECM
UAE	− 0.0084 (0.0071)	− 0.0172 (0.0063)	− 0.0011 (0.0001)	− 0.9286 (0.0000)
Kuwait	− 0.0066 (0.0000)	− 0.0228 (0.0000)	− 0.0010 (0.0000)	− 0.8135 (0.0001)
KSA	0.0102 (0.0001)	− 0.01791 (0.0001)	− 0.0019 (0.0010)	− 0.7440 (0.0000)
Oman	0.0052 (0.0000)	0.0097 (0.0010)	0.0075 (0.0000)	− 0.2865 (0.0001)
Bahrain	− 0.0312 (0.000)	− 0.0988 (0.0000)	0.0509 (0.0000)	− 0.4039 (0.0000)
Qatar	0.0293 (0.0000)	0.0586 (0.0007)	− 0.0875 (0.0000)	− 0.4589 (0.0001)

Table 5 shows the cross-country effect of stock market returns and COVID-19 of Gulf countries. It can be concluded that if the error correction term shows a negative indication with significant results, then it will be considered as the relationship will have long-run relationship, whereas the if variables show negative but not significant, indicating that countries will have short-term relationship. If the term shows no negative indication with significant or insignificant values, then these countries do not support either of the relationships.

From Table 5, it was observed that all the Gulf countries showed a long-term relationship between stock market returns and COVID-19 effect. While considering the individual countries effect all the three variables chosen the study found significant relationship with stock market returns, it shows all the gulf countries stock market return have impacted by novel coronavirus pandemic.

Table 6 presents the bivariate causality outcomes of confirmed cases and death counts of COVID-19 on stock market returns. The study found that there was a bi-directional causality relationship between death cases to stock market returns as well as confirmed cases of the disease to stock market returns, indicating an increase in the death rates will directly affect the stock returns and also reducing the stock returns with the death cases of COVID-19. The study also found that there was a uni-directional relationship of confirmed cases of COVID-19 and oil prices in GCC impacting the stock market returns, which shows that increasing confirmed cases affect the investment in stock market which also reduces the oil prices during the study period. Overall, it was observed that all the said variables found causing to affect the stock market returns may be considered as the influential factors for COVID-19.

5 Conclusion and Policy Implications

The main aim of this study was to examine the dual-shock effect of COVID-19 and oil prices and stock market returns of GCC. As the demand and supply shock of oil has

Table 6 Results of panel Granger causality test

	SR	*OP*	*CC*	*CD*	Results
SR		0.5716 (0.5635)	3.1518 (0.0037)	0.3455 (0.0082)	Bi-directional SR ↔ CC SR ↔ CD Uni-directional OP → CC
OP	0.0053 (0.9947)		0.5540 (0.5750)	0.1899 (0.8271)	
CC	15.7815 (0.0002)	3.5918 (0.0283)		1.6338 (0.1972)	
CD	0.1474 (0.0030)	0.0237 (0.9765)	3.1797 (0.8713)		

disrupted the global economy with the impact of COVID-19, this study attempts to trace out the relationship existence between these variables. To investigate the effect of this pandemic on oil prices and stock returns, the study employed a panel regression approach using two measurements: (1) daily growth in total confirmed cases and (2) daily growth in total deaths caused by COVID-19. From the results of panel co-integration and cross-country analysis, it was witnessed that there existed a long-term relationship between the variables under study which provides a conclusion that there was a strong impact of the pandemic and plunge of oil prices on the stock returns of GCC. In addition, when evaluated the COVID-19 confirmed cases and death cases, it was noted that 1% increase in oil price leads to a rise in the growth of stock market returns by 0.22%. Similarly, 1% change in the growth of confirmed cases leads to change 0.35% to the stock market returns. The table also found that 1% change in the death cases of COVID-19 leads to change in the growth of stock market returns by 0.11%. Thus, the study provides important information and policy implications for investors, portfolio managers and policy-makers to take actions and diversify the investments so as to avoid any future downfalls in the market.

Worldwide, central banks have initiated monetary policy changes to curb the downfall of the stock market indices in response to this pandemic. But federal governments have their role to match the fiscal measures with the monetary policy changes. Any hesitation in this respect can dilute their impact. The bidirectional relationship between the mortality rates and the stock returns strongly suggest that any further deterioration of the pandemic can undermine the positive effects of the measures already in place. The relationship between confirmed cases of COVID-19 and oil prices though unidirectional also bear similar policy implications. Further, insights from the study suggest that central banks and governments have to vigilantly watch the financial markets, to initiate reconciliatory actions, if a 'second wave' of COVID-19 occurs as feared by many international health agencies including the World Health Organization. Also many of the GCC members have announced economic support scheme and stimulus packages across the country to enhance liquidity and reduce the impact of the current global economic situation. A prediction is merely impossible as this pandemic continues to spread across; thus, health, humanitarian and socio-economic policies will have to be implemented for a quick and strong recovery.

References

Alam, Maqsood. 2020. Corrected middle east stocks-major middle east indexes decline on corona virus impact, Market News, March 15, 2020.

Al-Awadhi, A.M., K. Al-Saifi, A. Al Awadhi, and S. Al- Hammadi. 2020. Death and contagious infectious diseases: Impact of the COVID-19. *Journal of Behavioral and Experimental Finance* 27: 1–5.

Aloui, R., R. Gupta, and S.M. Miller. 2016. Uncertainty and crude oil returns. *Energy Economics* 55: 92–100.

Antonakakis, N., I. Chatziantoniou, and G. Filis. 2013. Dynamic co-movements of stock market returns, implied volatility and policy uncertainty. *Economics Letters* 120: 87–92.

Arabiannews.com. 2020. Gulf bourses feel impact of corona virus as oil prices dip below $50, March 1 2020. https://www.arabianbusiness.com/middle-east-markets/441596-gulf-bourses-feel-impact-of-coronavirus-as-oil-prices-dip-below-50.

Arshiyan, S., A. Chaker, and Y. Larisa. 2020. COVID-19 pandemic, oil prices, stock market, geopolitical risk and policy uncertainty nexus in the US economy: fresh evidence from the wavelet-based approach. International Review of Financial Analysis. Published online 2020 May 15. https://doi.org/10.1016/j.irfa.2020.101496.

Baker, S., N. Bloom, S.J. Davis, and S.J. Terry. 2020. COVID-19 Induced Economic Uncertainty. Paper available on the link: http://www.policyuncertainty.com/media/COVID--Induced%20.pdf. 04 April 2020.

Balcilar, M., R. Demirer, and S. Hammoudeh. 2019. Quantile relationship between oil and stock returns: Evidence from emerging and frontier stock markets. *Energy Policy* 134: 110931.

Barro, R.J., and J.F. Ursúa. 2008. Macroeconomic crises since 1870. *Brookings Papers on Economic Activity* 39: 255–350.

Basher, S.A., and P. Sadorsky. 2016. Hedging emerging market stock prices with oil, gold, VIX, and bonds: A comparison between DCC, ADCC and GO-GARCH. *Energy Economics* 54: 235–247.

Breitung, J. 2000. The local power of some unit root tests for panel data. *Advances in Econometrics* 15: 161–177. http://dx.doi.org/10.1016/S0731-9053(00)15006-6

Campbell Harvey "The Economic and Financial Implications of COVID-19". 2020. The Mayo Center for Asset Management at the University of Virginia Darden School of Business and the Financial Management Association International virtual seminars series. https://www.darden.virginia.edu/mayo-center/events/virtual-speaker-series.

Chinanews.com. 2020. Year of the rat market opens with 3177 A-shares hit their daily downside limits, 20 billion yuan foreign funds were buying low. 3 February 2020.

Das, D., S.B. Kumar, A.K. Tiwari, M. Shahbaz, and H.M. Hasim. 2018. On the relationship of gold, crude oil, stocks with financial stress: A causality-in-quantiles approach. *Finance Research Letters* 27: 169–174.

Donadelli, M., R. Kizys, and M. Riedel. 2016. Dangerous infectious diseases: Bad news for Main Street, good news for Wall Street? *Journal of Financial Markets* 35: 84–103.

Granger, C.W.J. 1969. Investigating causal relations by econometric models and cross-spectral methods. *Econometrica* 36: 424–438.

Im, K.S., M.H. Pesaran, and Y. Shin. 2003. Testing for unit roots in heterogeneous panels. *Journal of Econometrics* 115: 53–74.

Kang, W., R.A. Ratti, and I.J.L. Vespignanpp. 2017. Oil price shocks and policy uncertainty: New evidence on the effects of US and non-US oil production. *Energy Economics* 66: 536–546.

Kaplanski, G., and H. Levy. 2010. Sentiment and stock prices: The case of aviation disasters. *Journal of Financial Economics* 95: 174–201.

Levin, A., C.F. Lin, and C.S.J. Chu. 2012. Unit root tests in panel data: Asymptotic and finite-sample properties. *Journal of Econometrics* 108: 1–24.

Narendra Nathan. 2020. Stock market hit by corona virus reasons for turmoil what equity investors should do now. Economic times, March 16, 2020

OECD. 2020. COVID-19 crisis Response in MENA Countries. 29 April 2020.

Petroni, P. 1999. Critical values for co-integration tests in heterogeneous panels with multiple regressors. *Oxford Bulletin of Economics and Statistics* 61: 653–670.

Yang, L. 2019. Connectedness of economic policy uncertainty and oil price shocks in a time domain perspective. *Energy Economics* 80: 219–233.

Zouaoui, M., G.J.M. Nouyrigat, and F. Beer. 2011. How does investor sentiment affect stock market crises? Evidence from panel data. *Financial Review* 46: 723–747.

http://finance.chinanews.com/cj/2020/02-03/9077187.shtml. Accessed 27 March 2020.

https://economictimes.indiatimes.com/wealth/invest/stock-market-hit-by-coronavirus-reasons-for-turmoil-what-equity-investors-should-do-now/articleshow/74623291.cms?utm_source=contentofinterest&utm_medium=text&utm_campaign=cppst.

https://read.oecd-ilibrary.org/view/?ref=129_129919-4li7bq8asv&title=COVID--19-Crisis-Response-in-MENA-Countries.

A Cooperative Game Approach for Solving Water Resources Allocation Problem

Assem Tharwat, Marwa Mostafa Sabry and Ihab El-Khodary

Abstract

In water resources allocation problem, different stakeholders are faced with conflicting objectives and an optimal allocation of shared water resources in water transfer projects became an important task, taking into account the utilities of the different stakeholders. In Iran, there is unevenly distribution of water resources as well as increasing water demands, which have brought a need to transfer water from the Karoon river basin to the Rafsanjan basin in central Iran. Therefore, cooperative game theory can be used to analyze these problems, taking the advantage of cooperative games in maximizing the total net benefit of the shared stakeholders as well as increasing the individual shares of the allocated water to each stakeholder. In this paper, two cooperative game models are developed for modeling efficient water allocation among water stakeholders in water allocation problems in southern Iran. The main objective is to reallocate the water resources to achieve an equitable way of distributing these benefits among the water stakeholders to let them have the economic incentives for cooperation. Depending on the type of cooperation and the nature of the payoffs values, a fuzzy and a stochastic cooperative models are presented. The results showed that the models are appropriate in modeling real-world uncertain problems and efficient in allocating benefits specifically when considering the stochastic nature for payoffs.

A. Tharwat (✉)
American University in the Emirates
Dubai, UAE
e-mail: assemtharwat@hotmail.com

M. M. Sabry · I. El-Khodary
Faculty of Computers and Artificial Intelligence,
Cairo University, Giza, Egypt
e-mail: m.sabry@fci-cu.edu.eg

I. El-Khodary
e-mail: e.elkhodary@fci-cu.edu.eg

Keywords

Cooperative games · Stochastic cooperative model · Fuzzy cooperative model · Benefit allocation · Water resources

1 Introduction

In water allocation problems, there are usually several stakeholders with different and conflicting objectives. These conflicts arise when several water users compete for a limited amount of water supply. To achieve equitable and efficient water allocation, this requires the cooperation of all stakeholders in sharing water resources. Thus, water allocation methodologies need to be established to maintain equitable and efficient water allocations at river basins level. Cooperative game theory was used to model this scenario of water resource allocation, taking the advantage of cooperative games in maximizing the total net benefit of the shared stakeholders as well as increasing the individual shares of the allocated water to each stakeholder.

The aim of this paper is developing two cooperative game models for water resources reallocation to achieve an equitable way of distributing these benefits among the water stakeholders to let them have the economic incentives for cooperation. Depending on the type of cooperation and the nature of the payoffs values, a fuzzy and a stochastic cooperative models are presented. These models are used to solve a case study of water allocation problem in Southern Iran, showing the higher benefits achieved from the cooperation of the water stakeholders.

The organization of this paper is as follows: Sect. 2 presents the related work for solving water resources allocation problems. Section 3 presents the fuzzy and stochastic cooperative models, respectively and the framework for these models. Implementation for these models on a real case study in Iran is carried out in Sect. 4. Sections 5 gives the main concluding remarks.

© The Author(s), under exclusive license to Springer Nature Switzerland AG 2024

A. Salman and A. Tharwat (eds.), *ICT for Engineering & Critical Infrastructures*,
Advances in Science, Technology & Innovation, https://doi.org/10.1007/978-3-031-49309-6_4

2 Related Work

"Several attempts in the literature have been done for studying water resources allocation problem. Kucukmehmetoglu (2009) established a methodology to measure the rational economic and political impacts of extensive reservoir projects throughout a basin, using both linear programming for calculating benefits of coalitions, and game theory concepts (core and Shapley value) for evaluating the impacts of reservoirs. Sadegh et al. (2010) and Sadegh and Kerachian (2011) developed a methodology based on crisp and fuzzy Shapley games for optimal allocation of interbasin water resources. In their methodology, some fuzzy coalitions were constituted, and the total net benefit of the system was reallocated to water users using fuzzy Shapley value game with crisp payoffs.

Mahjouri and Ardestani (2010) developed a new game theoretic methodology for interbasin water transfer management to supply the competing users in a fair way, while the efficiency and environmental sustainability criteria were satisfied and the utilities of water users were incorporated. Mahjouri and Ardestani (2011) developed two cooperative and non-cooperative methodologies for a large-scale water allocation problem in Southern Iran. The water shares of the water users and their net benefits were determined using optimization models having economic objectives with respect to the physical and environmental constraints of the system.

Sadegh and Kerachian (2011) developed two new solution concepts for fuzzy cooperative games with crisp characteristic functions, namely Fuzzy Least Core and Fuzzy Weak Least Core. They aimed for optimal allocation of available water resources and associated benefits to water users in a river basin. Review of the previous works shows that the applicability and efficiency of cooperative games with fuzzy characteristic functions and fuzzy coalitions in modeling water resource allocation problems have not been yet investigated. Nikoo et al. (2012) developed a new methodology based on interval optimization and game theory for optimal operation of an interbasin water transfer system considering efficiency, equity and sustainability criteria. They proposed a linear version of the agricultural water production function and used it for incorporating deficit irrigation."

3 Proposed Models

In this section, two game models are proposed. Depending on the type of cooperation between water stakeholders whether partial or full cooperation, and the type of payoffs values whether fuzzy or stochastic random variables, a fuzzy or stochastic cooperative game models is determined. In the following, the details of developing both models are explained.

3.1 A Fuzzy Cooperative Game Model

In the fuzzy game model, water users could participate in forming the fuzzy grand coalition with a different participation rates, and therefore, they need not to use all of their initial water shares in the grand coalition. Also, handling the nature of the payoffs values as fuzzy numbers with known membership functions. A closed form formula in this model is developed that optimally allocates the payoffs among the cooperating players.

Taking imprecision of information in decision-making problems into account, a fuzzy characteristic function (i.e., fuzzy coalition value) can be incorporated into a cooperative game, represented by fuzzy numbers ω. Therefore, the characteristic function of such a game associates a crisp coalition with a fuzzy number $\omega(S)$. Assessing such fuzzy numbers for any crisp coalition S, a cooperative game with crisp coalitions and fuzzy characteristic function is defined by a pair (N, ω), where the fuzzy characteristic function ω: $P(N) \rightarrow \mathfrak{R}^{+} = \{\tilde{r} \in \mathfrak{R} | \tilde{r} \geq 0\}$ is such that $\omega(\varphi)=0$, (where $\mathfrak{R}$ is the fuzzy real line).

A fuzzy cooperative game (FCGame), i.e., with fuzzy coalitions and fuzzy characteristic function, is a pair $(N, \tilde{\omega})$ where N is the set of players with $i \in N=\{1, \ldots, n\}$ and the fuzzy characteristic function $\tilde{\omega}$: $U \rightarrow \mathfrak{R}$ for all $U \subseteq N$, such that $\omega(\varphi)=0$. A fuzzy coalition U is a fuzzy subset of N, which is a vector $U = \{U(1), \ldots, U(n)\}$ with coordinates $U(i)$ contained in the interval [0,1]. The number $U(i)$ indicates the membership grade of i in U. The class of all fuzzy subsets of U is denoted by $F(N)$. For a fuzzy subset U, , the α–level set is defined as: $[U]_{\alpha}=\{i \in N \mid U(i) \geq \alpha\}$, and the support set is denoted by $\text{supp}(U)=\{i \in N \mid U(i)>0\}$ (Borkotokey 2008).

Let $x(U)=(x_1(U), \ldots, x_n(U))$ be the payoff vector, such that $x_i(U)$ is the payoff of player i of the fuzzy coalition $U \in F(N)$. Since all players of coalition U cooperate together to maximize their profit, a linear multi-objective programming model can be formulated for any fuzzy coalition $U \in F(N)$ as follows (Tharwat et al. 2011):

Max $(w_1 x_1(U), w_2 x_2(U), \ldots, w_n x_n(U))$

Subject to

$$\begin{aligned} &\sum_{i \in \text{Supp}(U)} x_i(\mathrm{U}) = \tilde{\omega}(U), \; i = 1, \ldots, n \\ &x_i(U) \geq [U(i) \cdot \tilde{\omega}(\{i\})], \; \forall i \in \text{supp}(U) \\ &x_i(U) = 0, \qquad \forall i \notin \text{supp}(U) \end{aligned} \tag{1}$$

where $w_i = \left[\tilde{\omega}(\mathrm{U}) - \tilde{\omega}(\mathrm{U} - \{i\})\right] / \tilde{\omega}(U)$.

From the above formulated model, a closed form formula is derived which directly solves fuzzy cooperative games as follows (Sabry et al. 2017):

$$
\begin{aligned}
x_i &= U(i)EV_i + \frac{EV'_U[EV'_U - EV'_{U-i}]}{\sum_{i=1}^{N}[EV'_U - EV'_{U-i}]} \\
&= U(i)EV_i + \frac{[EV'_U - EV'_{U-i}]}{2EV'_U \sum_{i=1}^{N} EV'_{U-i}}
\end{aligned} \tag{2}
$$

where $EV_U = \frac{E_1^U + E_2^U}{2}$ is the expected value for the fuzzy worth $\widetilde{\omega}(U)$.

The developed closed form formula efficiently calculates the payoff distribution among the coalition players through transforming the payoff value of player i and the expected value of the fuzzy worth.

Proposition 1 *The payoffs of players obtained by solving the derived formula satisfy both the individual and the group rationality.*

Proposition 2 *Zero player (Null player) receives zero gain.*

3.2 A Stochastic Cooperative Game Model

In stochastic cooperative games, the payoff values are often estimations or approximations of reality. Under a stochastic environment, the value of the grand coalition, i.e., the total profit (or cost) is not given explicitly; rather it is represented as random variable knowing only its probability distribution.

This section presents a stochastic multi-objective optimization model that is developed to deal with stochastic cooperative games. Our research work handled the uncertainties through stochastic payoff functions through the presence of some random variables $\widetilde{v}\ (s)$ with known distribution functions, $F_{\widetilde{v}(s)}(x) = P\left\{\widetilde{v}\ (s) \le x\right\}$. Under stochastic cooperative game (SCG), a pair of sets SCG $= (I, \widetilde{v})$ is used, where $I = \{1 \ldots n\}$: the set of players; $\widetilde{v}(S)$: incomes (worth) of coalitions $S \subset I$, that are random variables with determined density functions $P_{\widetilde{v}(s)}(x)$ (Suijs et al. 1999; Ma et al. 2008). Thus, a multi-objective chance constrained programming model can be formulated for any coalition with stochastic worth as follows (Tharwat et al. 2019):

$$
\begin{aligned}
&\text{Max} \quad x_1(\alpha), x_2(\alpha), \ldots, x_n(\alpha) \\
&\text{Subject to} \\
&\quad \frac{3B_i}{3 - B_i^2} e^{-B_{i/2}^2} \ge \sqrt{\frac{\pi}{2}}(2y_i + 1), \quad i = 1, \ldots, I \\
&\quad \frac{3\delta}{3 - \delta^2} e^{-\frac{\delta^2}{2}} \ge \sqrt{\frac{\pi}{2}}(2z + 1) \\
&\quad x_i(\alpha) - B_i\sigma\left[\tilde{v}(\mathrm{i})\right] \ge E\left[\tilde{v}(\mathrm{i})\right], \quad i = 1, \ldots, I \\
&\quad \sum_{i=1}^{I} x_i(\alpha) - \delta\sigma\left[\tilde{v}(I)\right] \le E\left[\tilde{v}(I)\right] \\
&\quad y_i \ge 1 - \alpha, \quad i = 1, \ldots, I \\
&\quad z \le \alpha \\
&\quad x_i(\alpha) \ge 0, \quad i = 1, \ldots, I \\
&\quad B_i, \delta \quad \text{are unrestricted in sign} \\
&\quad 0 \le y_i,\ z \le 1
\end{aligned} \tag{3}
$$

where $E\left[\tilde{v}(i)\right]$, $\sigma\left[\tilde{v}(i)\right]$ and $E\left[\tilde{v}(I)\right]$, $\sigma\left[\tilde{v}(I)\right]$ are the mean and standard deviation of the normal random variables $\tilde{v}(i)$ and $\tilde{v}(I)$, respectively. B_i and δ are the inverse cumulative distribution function of the standard normal random variable $\tilde{v}(i)$ at y_i and $\tilde{v}(I)$ at z, respectively.

Proposition 1 *Efficiency: The payoff vector of the model provides efficiency as the total payoff of the grand coalition is distributed to all cooperating players.*

Proposition 2 *Fairness: The payoff vector provides fairness among all cooperating players as it allocates higher share to the player whose individual contribution is higher than another.*

Proposition 3 *Existence and Uniqueness: The solution of the developed stochastic multi-objective optimization model always exists as the model is converged to the optimal solution based on the derived convergence constraints and provide unique allocation vector.*

Proposition 4 *Complexity: The number of constraints increases linearly with the number of cooperating players and not exponentially like Shapley value.*

3.3 Framework of the Model

In this section, a general flowchart of the proposed models is illustrated in Fig. 1.

4 Case Study

In Iran, there is unevenly distribution of water resources due to precipitation. In central Iran, there is low rate of precipitation and increasing water demands, which have led to high usage on the groundwater resources, which are the only dependable water resources in this region. As such, recently, there is a need to transfer water from the Karoon river basin in southwestern Iran to the Rafsanjan basin in central Iran. Two important rivers are the main branches to the Karoon river basin, the Karoon and Dez. These two rivers connect together and form the huge Karoon river that ends in the Persian Gulf. The Karoon and Dez rivers represent the main sources of water for supplying the agricultural and agro-industrial users.

According to Mahab-Ghods Consulting Engineers (2004), the total water demand and need of the Karoon river basin is 24.9 billion cubic meters while the total discharge (supply) of the great Karoon river is 20.4 billion cubic meters. This statement showed that Karoon river basin had major problems in supplying its own water demands in some months of the year particularly in dry years. One of the most important streams of the great Karoon river is the Solegan river. Its average flow is 26 m^3/s. The Iran Water Resources Management Company (IWRMC) had planned to construct Solegan reservoir (dam) on this river to make the opportunity to allocate water to the Rafsanjan plain area in central Iran. The Rafsanjan basin has an annual average precipitation rate of 170 mm, where groundwater resources are the only dependable water resources in this basin, as its rivers are seasonal and their annual discharge are insignificant (shortage is about one million cubic meters) (Fig. 2).

Therefore, IWRMC had decided to supply the water demands of this basin by transferring 250 million cubic meters of water from the Solegan river annually. This

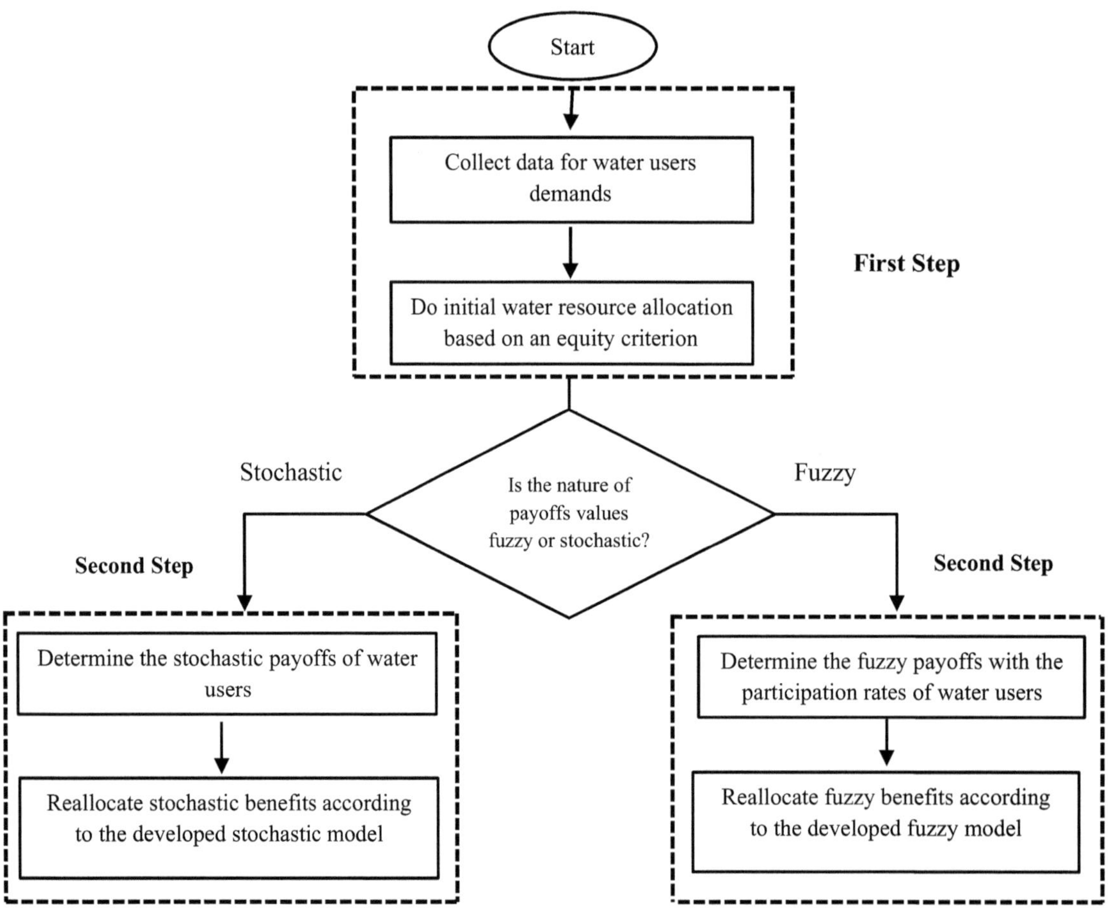

Fig. 1 Framework of the proposed models

transferred amount was used to supply the shortage demands and at the same time protected the groundwater resources in Rafsanjan basins."

A secondary data was given over a 5-year plan horizon, and the average monthly water demands for the water users were estimated. Table 1 shows the main water demands (players) which are Rafsanjan agricultural sector in the Rafsanjan basin, Khuzestan local agricultural sector in the Karoon basin, Khuzestan modern agro-industrial sector and finally Khuzestan old agro-industrial sector.

As an initial step, an optimization model was used to determine the initial water allocation shares for all users (players). These allocations are proportional to the shares allocated by the government, which are based on an equity criterion. These are the monthly shares with respect to the legal water supply rights and the reservoir physical and environmental constraints. Because the benefits were calculated yearly, the monthly water allocated shares were converted to the annual ones to be applicable in the calculations of the characteristic functions (Abed Elmdoust and Kerachian 2012). The results of this step were used as inputs to the second step.

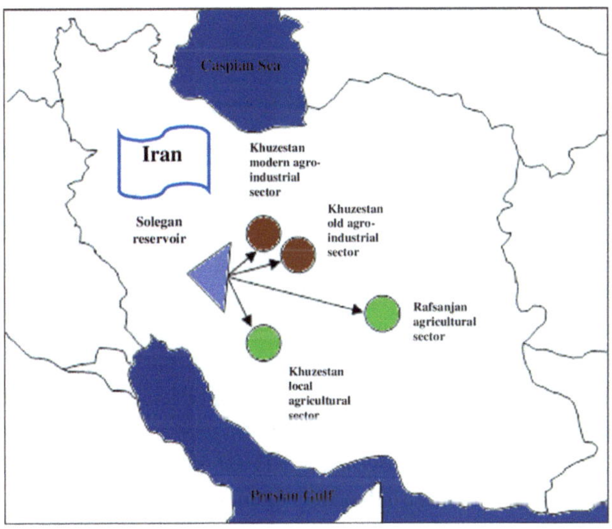

Fig. 2 Solegan reservoir and water demand sectors (Nikoo et al. 2012)

4.1 Implementing the Developed Models

The closed form formula for fuzzy cooperative games and the stochastic model developed earlier in Sect. 3 are implemented in this section on the water allocation problem of Southern Iran. A comparison between these implementations are discussed at the end of this section.

4.1.1 A Fuzzy Scenario for Water Allocation

The fuzzy game model allows water users to participate in forming the fuzzy grand coalition with a different participation rates and therefore; they need not to use all of their initial water shares in the grand coalition. In addition, the worth for the formed coalitions is uncertain fuzzy values. The net benefit coefficients and the capacity of each water user, presented in Table 2, are used to calculate the fuzzy worth of each possible crisp coalition. These fuzzy worth of each of the formed crisp coalitions are shown in Table 3.

Thus, from the calculated fuzzy worth of coalitions and the participation rates of each user given in Table 4, the total fuzzy worth of the fuzzy grand coalition was determined using the Choquet integral form function for fuzzy games, (Tsurumi et al, 2001) as follows:

Table 1 Main water demands for all users (million m^3)

Month	Rafsanjan agricultural sector	Khuzestan local agricultural sector	Khuzestan modern agro-industrial sector	Khuzestan old agro-industrial sector
April	17	18.8	2.1	2.5
May	39.8	24.8	2.7	3.3
June	49.6	27	3	3.6
July	47	34.2	3.8	4.6
August	45	30.4	3.4	4
September	38	25	2.7	3.3
October	28.2	15.4	1.7	2.1
November	8.8	9	1	1.2
December	0.2	6.2	0.7	0.9
January	0	5.6	0.6	0.8
February	0	6.6	0.7	0.9
March	1.2	13.8	1.5	1.9
Annual Demand	274.8	216.8	24.1	28.9

$$t\tilde{\omega}(\{1,2,3,4\}) = \sum_{m=1}^{q(K)} \tilde{\omega}([K]_{r_m}) \cdot (r_m - r_{m-1}) \\ = (102.44, 102.53, 103.23) \times 10^5\$ \tag{4}$$

Solving this fuzzy model with our developed formula for fuzzy games:

Step 1: Defuzzifying the total coalitional worth.
$EV_N = 102.68 \times 10^5\$$

Step 2: Calculating ($EV_{N-i'}$) for all sub-coalitions and $EV_{N'}$

$N - i$	{2,3,4}	{1,3,4}	{1,2,4}	{1,2,3}	{1,2,3,4}
$EV(\times 10^5\$)$	91.7	95.54	23.75	27.6	102.68
$EV\prime(\times 10^5\$)$	59.59	62.9	12.37	0.08	68.13

Step 3: Finding the individual's profit shares by applying the formula.

Players (i)	1	2	3	4
	Khuzestan modern	Khuzestan old	Khuzestan local	Rafsanjan
$(\times 10^5\$)$	6.2	4.5	50.79	42.39

4.1.2 A Stochastic Scenario for Water Allocation

In the stochastic cooperative game model, water users fully cooperate in the grand coalition with all of their resources, but the coalitional worth in this case is considered normal random variable determined by the net benefit coefficients, $\boldsymbol{BC(N)}$, and the capacity of each water user, $\boldsymbol{c(i,m)}$, shown in Table 5.

The stochastic worth of each of the formed crisp sub-coalitions were as follows ($\times 10^5\$$):

Given the four water users will cooperate together sharing all their resources with the stochastic coalitional worth. They want be sure that the total worth is enough to allocate the profit allocation by at least 95%.

Formulating this scenario as stochastic cooperative game, and following our developed model, the obtained deterministic programming problem for the multi-objective stochastic problem will be:

$$\text{Max} \quad 0.4x_1(\alpha), 0.5x_2(\alpha), 3.6x_3(\alpha), 3.1x_4(\alpha)$$

Subject to

$$x_1 - 0.7\beta_1 \geq 5.2$$
$$x_2 - 0.7\beta_2 \geq 5.6$$
$$x_4 - 0.4\beta_4 \geq 13.5$$
$$\sum_{i=1}^{4} x_i(\alpha) - 8.7\delta \leq 211$$
$$\frac{3\beta_i}{3-\beta_i^2} e^{-\beta_{i/2}^2} \geq \sqrt{\frac{\pi}{2}}(2y_i + 1), \quad i = 1, \ldots, 4$$
$$\frac{3\delta}{3-\delta^2} e^{-\frac{\delta^2}{2}} \geq \sqrt{\frac{\pi}{2}}(2z + 1)$$
$$y_i \geq 0.95, \quad i = 1, \ldots, 4$$
$$z \leq 0.05$$
$$0 \leq y_i, z \leq 1, \; x_i(\alpha) \geq 0, \quad i = 1, \ldots, 4$$
$$\beta_i, \delta \quad \text{are unrestricted in sign}$$

4.2 Discussion and Comparison of Results

In the developed closed form fuzzy formula, the profit shares for the water stakeholders are distributed in accordance with the product of the participation rates and the individual worth for each stakeholder. Figure 3 shows the allocation of profit shares for each water user that resulted from applying the developed fuzzy formula.

Comparing these obtained values with those obtained using the Hukuhara–Shapley value (Abed Elmdoust and Kerachian 2012):

Players (i)	1	2	3	4
	Khuzestan modern	Khuzestan old	Khuzestan local	Rafsanjan
$(\times 10^5\$)$	6.67	4.52	49.57	40.73

Revealed that the developed formula increased the percentages of the profit shares for stakeholders whose participation rates are higher, which is not the case when solving using the Hukuhara–Shapley Value. Figure 4 shows that the percentages of profit for Khuzestan Local and Rafsanjan were increased to 48.5% and 42.3% respectively using the developed formula against Shapley value that yielded 48.4% and 41.4%, respectively. For Khuzestan

Table 2 Net benefit coefficient $bc(i)$ and the annual capacity $c(i)$ of users

Players (i)	1	2	3	4
	Khuzestan modern	Khuzestan old	Khuzestan local	Rafsanjan
$bc(i)$ ($/m^3)	0.31	0.28	0.27	1.07
$c(i)$ (m^3)	24.1×10^6	28.9×10^6	216.8×10^6	274.8×10^6

Table 3 Fuzzy worth of each of the formed crisp coalition

Coalitions	Fuzzy payoffs	Coalitions	Fuzzy payoffs	Coalitions	Fuzzy payoffs
$\omega(\{1\})$	(4.6, 5.1, 5.9)	$\omega(\{1, 3\})$	(45.6, 50.7, 58.3)	$\omega(\{1, 2, 3\})$	(51.1, 56.8, 65.3)
$\omega(\{2\})$	(5, 5.5, 6.4)	$\omega(\{1, 4\})$	(27.9, 31, 35.7)	$\omega(\{1, 2, 4\})$	(46.7, 51.9, 59.7)
$\omega(\{3\})$	(34.5, 38.6, 42.8)	$\omega(\{2, 3\})$	(42.3, 46.9, 54)	$\omega(\{1, 3, 4\})$	(167.9, 186.7, 214.7)
$\omega(\{4\})$	(13.2, 13.5, 13.9)	$\omega(\{2, 4\})$	(30.9, 34.4, 39.6)	$\omega(\{2, 3, 4\})$	(171, 190, 218.5)
$\omega(\{1, 2\})$	(10.1, 11.2, 12.9)	$\omega(\{3, 4\})$	(152.3, 169.2, 194.6)	$\omega(\{1, 2, 3, 4\})$	(186.7, 207.5, 238.7)

Table 4 Participation rate of each water user in the formed fuzzy grand coalition

Players (i)	1	2	3	4
	Khuzestan modern	Khuzestan old	Khuzestan local	Rafsanjan
Participation rate	0.53	0.47	0.86	0.63

Table 5 Stochastic worth for all sub-coalitions of water players

Coalitions	Stochastic payoffs	Coalitions	Stochastic payoffs	Coalitions	Stochastic payoffs
$\tilde{v}(\{1\})$	$N(5.2,0.7)$	$\tilde{v}(\{1, 3\})$	$N(51.5,6.4)$	$\tilde{v}(\{1, 2, 3\})$	$N(57.7,7.1)$
$\tilde{v}(\{2\})$	$N(5.6,0.7)$	$\tilde{v}(\{1, 4\})$	$N(31.5,3.9)$	$\tilde{v}(\{1, 2, 4\})$	$N(52.7,6.5)$
$\tilde{v}(\{3\})$	$N(38.6,4.2)$	$\tilde{v}(\{2, 3\})$	$N(47.7,5.9)$	$\tilde{v}(\{1, 3, 4\})$	$N(189.7,23.6)$
$\tilde{v}(\{4\})$	$N(13.5,0.4)$	$\tilde{v}(\{2, 4\})$	$N(34.9,4.4)$	$\tilde{v}(\{2, 3, 4\})$	$N(193.1,23.9)$
$\tilde{v}(\{1, 2\})$	$N(11.4,1.4)$	$\tilde{v}(\{3, 4\})$	$N(172.03,21.3)$	$\tilde{v}(\{1, 2, 3, 4\})$	$N(210.9,26.2)$

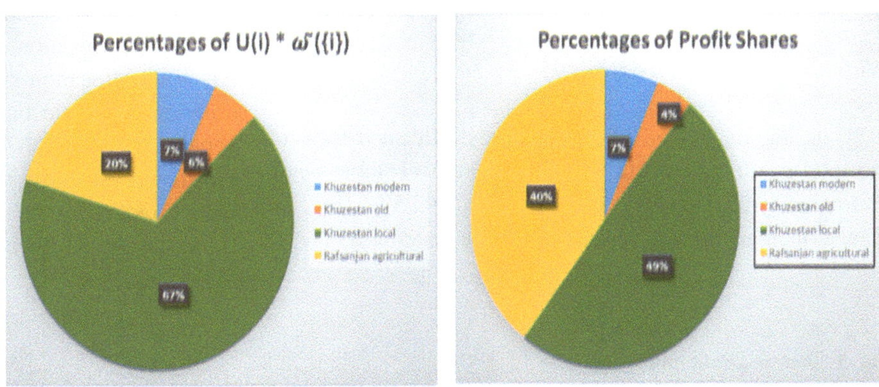

Fig. 3 Percentages of profit shares distribution with the participation rates using the developed formula

Modern and Khuzestan Old, the formula resulted in 5.4% and 3.7% respectively while Shapley value resulted in 6.3 and 3.9%. Thus, the allocation vector resulted from the developed formula reallocated the coalitional worth more efficiently than Hukuhara–Shapley value with less computational effort (no need to calculate crisp Shapley values at the very beginning) and overcoming the Hukuhara conditions.

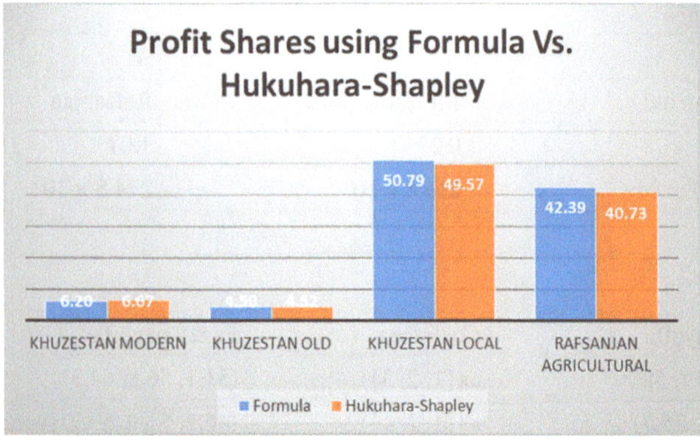

Fig. 4 Profit shares using the developed formula versus Hukuhara–Shapley value

On the other hand, when solving the water allocation problem using the developed stochastic model, the individual profit shares for the water users will be:

	1 Khuzestan modern	2 Khuzestan old	3 Khuzestan local	4 Rafsanjan
($\times 10^5$\$)	26.47	35.93	96.93	47.36

With total coalitional worth = 206.69 ($\times 10^5$\$)

When solving the same stochastic model using Shapley value, the allocated payoffs were:

	1 Khuzestan modern	2 Khuzestan old	3 Khuzestan local	4 Rafsanjan
($\times 10^5$\$)	24.68	31.46	93.68	45.38

With total coalitional worth = 195.2 ($\times 10^5$\$)

Thus, the developed stochastic model allocated 97% of the total coalitional worth, which is more acceptable when compared with Shapley that allocated 92.5% (Fig. 5). Hence, increasing the profit shares for the water users.

Comparisons of results obtained from applying the fuzzy and stochastic game models revealed that applying the stochastic environment and considering the water demands of the water users as stochastic random variables rather than the fuzzy nature for them (as previously considered by other researchers; Abed Elmdoust and Kerachian 2012), achieved efficient and higher profit shares allocations for stakeholders which increased the overall benefit and the individual ones. The major economic benefit achieved when transferring highest water share to Khuzestan local agricultural sector, which resulted in stabilizing and preserving the underground water condition in this area.

5 Conclusions

In this paper, two cooperative game models are developed for modeling efficient water allocation among water stakeholders in water allocation problem. In Southern Iran, there is unevenly distribution of water resources that requires transfer of water resources from basins to another. A fuzzy cooperative game model was developed in which a closed form formula was used to reallocate benefits between water stakeholders. A second scenario of stochastic cooperative game modeling in which the benefits are considered stochastic random variables was used to achieve higher allocations between water stakeholders. The main objective is to reach higher overall net benefit and to achieve an equitable way of distributing these benefits among the water stakeholders that is fair enough to let them have the economic incentives to cooperate forming the grand coalition. The approach for these models consists of two steps. In the first step, an optimization model was used to determine the initial water allocation shares for all users based on an equity criterion. In the second step, water users form coalitions to benefit from cooperation and depending on the nature of payoff values, either the fuzzy or the stochastic model was used to reallocate the benefits in an efficient way. The results showed that the developed fuzzy model is more effective

Fig. 5 Percentages of profit shares using the developed stochastic model versus Shapley value

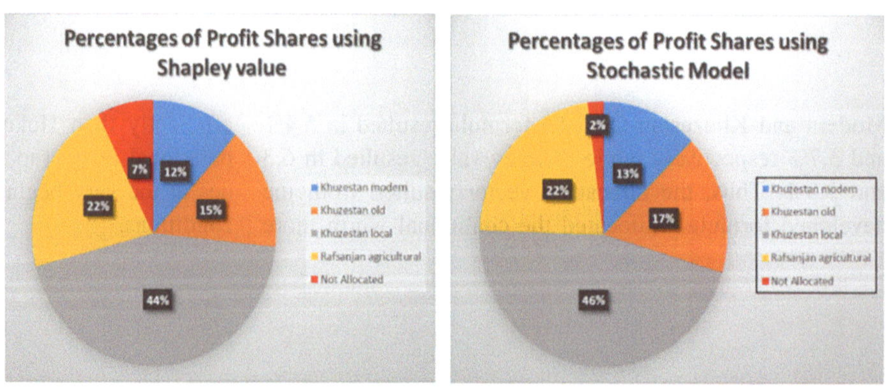

than Hukuhara–Shapley function overcoming its limitation with less computational effort. In addition, applying the developed stochastic model achieved more benefits between water stakeholders than the fuzzy scenario to reach an early assumption that the stochastic nature for the benefits is more realistic than assuming the fuzzy ones. The proposed approach allows applying both fuzzy and stochastic scenarios for solving water allocation problems, though real implementations revealed that considering the stochastic nature for stakeholder payoffs are more beneficial than the fuzzy ones.

References

Abed Elmdoust, A., and R. Kerachian. 2012. Water resources allocation using a cooperative game with fuzzy payoffs and fuzzy coalitions. *Water Resources Management* 26 (13): 3961–3976.

Borkotokey, S. 2008. Cooperative games with fuzzy coalitions and fuzzy characteristic functions. *Fuzzy Sets and Systems* 159: 138–151.

Ghods, M. 2004. Supplementary Environmental and Social Assessment of Alborz Intergrated Land and Water. *Mahab Ghods Consulting Engineers: Tehran, Iran*, 248.

Kucukmehmetoglu, M. 2009. A game theoretic approach to assess the impacts of major investments on transboundary water resources: The case of the Euphrates and Tigris. *Water Resources Management* 23 (15): 3069.

Ma, Y., Z. Gao, W. Li, N. Jiang, and L. Guo. 2008. The shapley value for stochastic cooperative game. *Modern Applied Science* 2 (4): 76.

Mahjouri, N., and M. Ardestani. 2010. A game theoretic approach for interbasin water resources allocation considering the water quality issues. *Environmental Monitoring and Assessment* 167 (1–4): 527–544.

Mahjouri, N., and M. Ardestani. 2011. Application of cooperative and non-cooperative games in large-scale water quantity and quality management: A case study. *Environmental Monitoring and Assessment* 172 (1–4): 157–169.

Nikoo, M.R., R. Kerachian, and H. Poorsepahy-Samian. 2012. An interval parameter model for cooperative inter-basin water resources allocation considering the water quality issues. *Water Resources Management* 26 (11): 3329–3343.

Sabry, M., A. Tharwat, and I. El-Khodary. 2017. Optimized formula for distributing coalition worth in n-person fuzzy cooperative games. *World Journal of Management* 8(1): 94–103. https://doi.org/10.21102/wjm.2017.03.81.07.

Sadegh, M., and R. Kerachian. 2011. Water resources allocation using solution concepts of fuzzy cooperative games: Fuzzy least core and fuzzy weak least core. *Water Resources Management* 25 (10): 2543–2573.

Sadegh, M., N. Mahjouri, and R. Kerachian. 2010. Optimal interbasin water allocation using crisp and fuzzy Shapley games. *Water Resources Management* 24 (10): 2291–2310.

Suijs, J., P. Borm, A. De Waegenaere, and S. Tijs. 1999. Cooperative games with stochastic payoffs. *European Journal of Operational Research* 113 (1): 193–205.

Tharwat, A., O. Soliman, I. Elkhodary, and M. Sabry. 2011. Linear Multi-Objective Model for Solving Fuzzy Cooperative Games.

Tharwat, A., M. Sabry, and I. El-Khodary. 2019. An optimization model for solving stochastic cooperative games. In *Creative Business and Social Innovations for a Sustainable Future*, 33–38. Cham: Springer.

Tsurumi, M., T. Tanino, and M. Inuiguchi. 2001. A Shapley function on a class of cooperative fuzzy games. *European Journal of Operational Research* 129: 596–618.

Dynamic Key Encryption Using the Embedded Three Pass Protocol for Securing TCP Streams in WiMAX Link

Suherman and Marwan Al-Akaidi

Abstract

This paper proposes embedded three pass protocol (TPP) for securing TCP streams through the worldwide interoperability microwave access (WiMAX) link. TPP messages are embedded into either WiMAX frame headers or TCP header to secure TCP connection. The embedded TPP in WiMAX MAC layer headers ensure any messages flow through WiMAX link is protected. Even though TCP packets experience average delay up to 47.8 ms, TCP streams are well protected as all signals are encrypted dynamically. On the other hand, by embedding the TPP messages into TCP header, TCP delay decreases significantly to about 29.4 ms. However, only TCP streams are protected. If existing WiMAX link security is sufficient, the later method is preferred. However, embedded TPP in TCP header has more security risks as TCP connection can be failed if other unprotected WiMAX signal is attacked and existing WiMAX security is weak. Multiple links connection prefers embedded TPP in TCP header as TCP streams are protected end to end.

Keywords

Embedded three pass protocol · WiMAX · TCP · Secure network

The original version of the chapter has been revised: The author "Marwan Al-Akaidi" affiliation has been updated. A correction to the chapter can be found at https://doi.org/10.1007/978-3-031-49309-6_8

Suherman
Universitas Sumatera Utara, Medan 20155, Indonesia

M. Al-Akaidi (✉)
Wigwe University, Isiokpo, Nigeria
e-mail: mmalakaidi@gmail.com

1 Introduction

Worldwide interoperability microwave access (WiMAX) provides high-speed link enabling TCP-based applications such as the commercial video streaming application served in a long range point-to-point, point-to-multipoint (IEEE Std. 802.16-2004 2004) and mobile wireless connection (IEEE Std. 802.16e-2005 2005). Since video streaming applications have been widely used for home or offices customers, wireless link security becomes important. WiMAX is superior to other wireless technologies despite its implementation in some countries is less popular than WiFi and 4G networks (IEEE Std 802.16m-2011 2011). However, since internet demands and its customers grow rapidly, other wireless technologies are not as competitive as WiMAX in term bandwidth availability.

WiMAX standards define features and services from data link level into application layer by introducing advanced physical and data link techniques as well as QoS negotiation and enforcement (Vu et al. 2010). In terms of security, WiMAX defines its security features in a specific security sublayer which is part of MAC layer (Ahson and Ilyas 2018). This sublayer is responsible for authorization, authentication and encryption of incoming and outgoing data. Base station (BS) imposes security policies for subscriber stations (SS) or mobile stations (MS). BS employs digital certificates, security association, privacy and key management, authorization and data encryption that complement the attribute of a specific type of services.

Authorization in WiMAX is performed by three authentication types: Rivest Shamir Adleman/RSA-based authentication, Extensible Authentication Protocol/EAP-based authentication and RSA-EAP-based authentication (Ahson and Ilyas 2018). Authentication in WiMAX requires SS/MS to request authentication key and a security association identity from BS. This request should contain X.509 certificate of SS, cryptographic ID and the selected encryption algorithms. BS replies the authentication key encrypted by a public key.

© The Author(s), under exclusive license to Springer Nature Switzerland AG 2024, corrected publication 2024
A. Salman and A. Tharwat (eds.), *ICT for Engineering & Critical Infrastructures*,
Advances in Science, Technology & Innovation, https://doi.org/10.1007/978-3-031-49309-6_5

Validation is made by using authentication authorization and accounting server (Sangwan and Singh 2017).

WiMAX uses five keys to secure communication: AK, key encryption key (KEK), downlink hash function-based message authentication code (HMAC) key, uplink HMAC key, and traffic encryption key (TEK). AK is used during authentication. KEK is for TEK encryption and distribution, downlink uplink hashed message authentication code (HMAC) is for data authentication of key distribution messages from the BS to the SS, and TEK is used for data encryption. After completing the authentication and initial key exchange, data transmissions between BS and SS are encrypted by using the traffic encryption key (TEK) for encryption (Simion et al. 2012).

However, some issues have been reported (Kumar et al. 2018). Potential threats include jamming, scrambling, water torture, forgery, masquerading and Denial of Service (DoS). Jamming introduces a strong noise source to reduce WiMAX channel capacity. Scrambling confuses WiMAX connections by interchanging connection identities (CIDs). Water torture consumes receiver's battery by resending legitimate WiMAX frames. Masquerading steals WiMAX authorities by means of spoofing and sniffing. Denial of Service (DoS) resends ranging request/response messages, mobile neighbor advertisement messages, fast power control messages, authorization-invalid messages and reset command messages frequently to either BS or SS (Simion et al. 2012). Some existing works that increased encryption strength within WiMAX have been proposed (Lakshmi 2017; Oguta 2018; Panda and Chattopadhyay 2019; Yadav et al. 2018; Alezabi et al. 2016).

Since transmission control protocol (TCP) dominates the internet traffics (Tian et al. 2005; Suherman and Al–Akaidi, M. 2014), it is urgent to guarantee TCP traffic security when flowing through network. This work examines the three pass protocol (TPP) implementation into either medium access layer or transport layer to provide dynamic encryption keys for securing TCP streams while maintaining TCP performances. In order to do so, an embedded three pass protocol (TPP) (Badawi and Zarlis 2019) in WiMAX frames headers as well as in TCP headers is proposed and compared. Security coverage and traffic delays are the main concern of the implementations.

2 Proposed Schema

2.1 The Embedded Three Pass Protocol Messages in MAC Layer

Three pass protocol (TPP) performs a secure key exchange using three message transfers. In order to efficiently transfer TPP messages, instead of treating TPP messages as WiMAX data, these messages should be inserted into medium access payloads. By doing this, TPP delay can be minimized. This paper chooses the WiMAX bandwidth request and MAP headers to piggyback these messages. Selection is based on the suitable flow schedule as TPP has three subsequent messages to perform the key exchange. Bandwidth request and MAP payload are suitable to do the tasks even though other signaling payloads are possible.

TPP implementation in this paper is referred to as embedded TPP. The process flow is shown in Fig. 1. Initially, the encryption key X for securing data is encrypted by using key A in subscriber station (SS). This message is put in bandwidth request field as a piggybacked data. Base station (BS) encrypts the received message using key B and transmitted back to SS through MAP message. SS decrypts the received message by using key A and sends the ciphertext to BS trough information piggybacking to BS. Finally, BS decrypts the message by using key B and gets the key X. Dynamic key is achieved by sending different keys for different bandwidth requests.

In addition, in order to ensure TPP message transfers have the highest successful probability, WiMAX payload that carries TPP messages employs the prioritized bandwidth request mechanism. There have been many bandwidth request schemas proposed, such as contention request with truncated binary exponential back off (TBEB), contention request with piggyback, unicast- and polling-based request (Al-Akaidi et al. 2012; Suherman et al. 2015), enhanced exponential increase exponential decrease (EIED)-based contention resolution (Anbazhagan and Rangaswamy 2013), utility-based backoff (UBB) (Thapa and Shin 2009) and enhanced unicast bandwidth requests (Xiong et al. 2020). The objective of bandwidth request schema in this paper is how to enhance successful probability of bandwidth request carrying the TPP messages.

In order to enhance bandwidth request mechanism that carrying TPP messages, reduced contention window is applied for bandwidth request mechanism. In TBEB (Chen and Tseng 2008), algorithm uses a random number chosen from interval $[0, W_{i-1}]$, where W stands for window size. Contention window size will be reduced for bandwidth request carrying the TPP messages. Window reduction is set 50% for TPP messages. The random number is chosen from the interval $[0, 0.05(W_{i-1})]$. In case bandwidth request message experiences collision, increment is set to $W_i = 2^{i-1} W_{i-1}$, $I \neq 0$, where $W_i = 0.5 W_i$.

The probability of a successful request, P_s is defined as a function of the slots s and the number of contending nodes, n_{exp} as in Eq. 1. With the expected contending arrival is defined as Poisson distributed, λ, and is affected by frame duration f, and the number of SS, n, the probability that one SS sends a bandwidth request is n_{tx}/n_{tf}. The average number of requests n_{tx}, and the average request processing time n_{tf}, are given in Eqs. 3 and 4 while c is collision probability.

Fig. 1 Proposed embedded TPP schema in WiMAX MAC layer

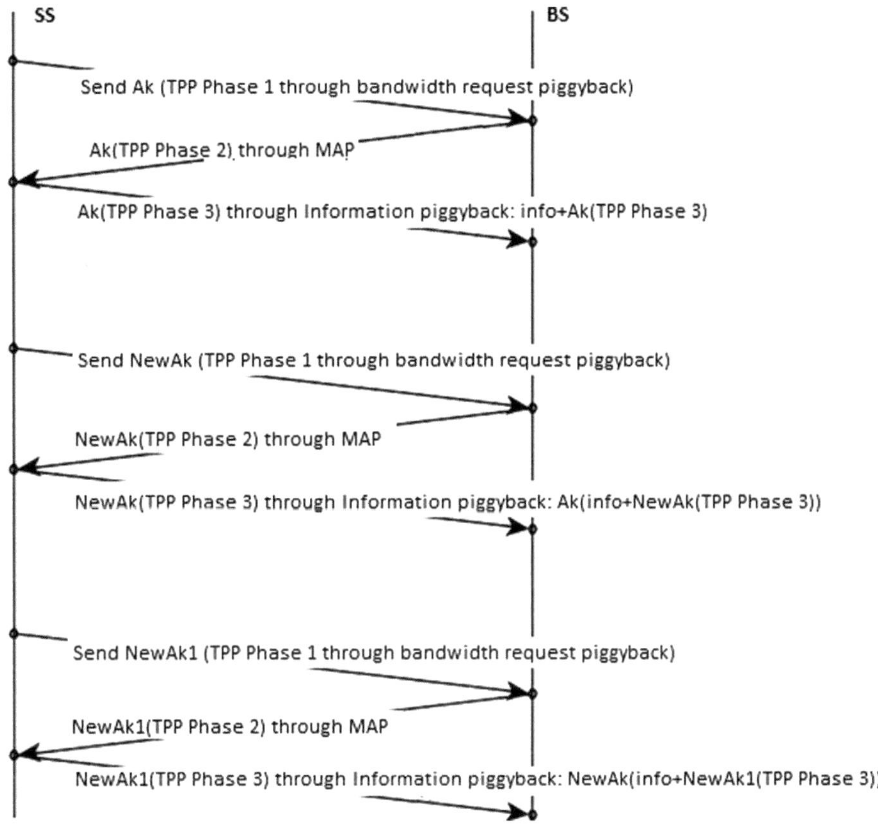

$$P_s = \left(\frac{s-1}{s}\right)^{n_{\exp-1}} \quad (1)$$

$$n_{\exp} = n\frac{n_{tx}}{n_{tf}}\left(1 - e^{-\lambda . n_{tf} f}\right) \quad (2)$$

$$n_{tx} = \sum_{i=1}^{m} i(1-c)c^{i-1} + (m+1)c^m \quad (3)$$

$$n_{tf} = \sum_{i=1}^{m}(1-c)c^{i-1}\left(\sum_{j=1}^{i}\frac{1}{W_j}\left(\sum_{k=1}^{W_j}k\right)\right) + c^m\left(\sum_{i=1}^{m+1}\frac{1}{W_i}\left(\sum_{j=1}^{W_i}j\right)\right) \quad (4)$$

2.2 The Embedded Three Pass Protocol Messages in TCP Header

Embedded TPP in TCP header has been previously discussed in Suherman et al. (2020). The three TPP messages are embedded in the TCP handshaking packets: SYN, SYN-ACK and ACK. Figure 2 describes the process. During the call establishment, encryption key Ak is sent by using TPP message 1, 2 and 3. Each message is transported by SYN, SYN-ACK and ACK subsequently.

In order to provide dynamic encryption key, the new encryption key can be inserted in acknowledgment packet. This acknowledgment packet is then encrypted by using the previous key. So that encryption key can be dynamically modified without requesting new TPP stage. There is no lower layer support to do this matter.

3 Evaluation Method

In order to show the effectiveness and the comparison of the methods, NS-2 simulations were performed. NIST WiMAX module (Mubarakah et al. 2018) was employed for simulating WiMAX network with BS transmit power is set to cover area in radius 1000 m using 64 QAM modulation and a two-ray ground propagation model. There were four simulated SSs with one evaluated SS using the proposed embedded TPP protocol. The simulated traffic was akiyo_cif.yuv video sent by using TCP with window size 1. The measured parameters are transmission delay and security coverage. Simulation configuration is shown in Fig. 3 and is modified later. RSA algorithm is employed for information encryption, while one-time pad (OTP) is for TPP encryption and decryption.

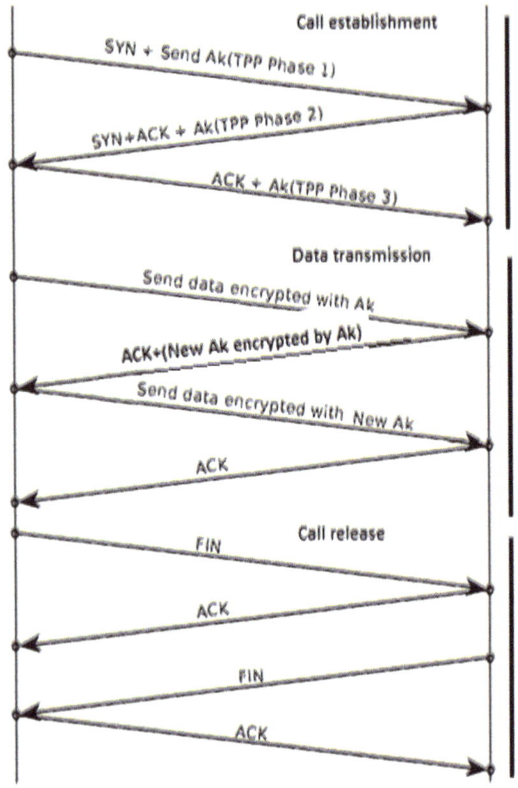

Fig. 2 Embedded TPP schema in TCP

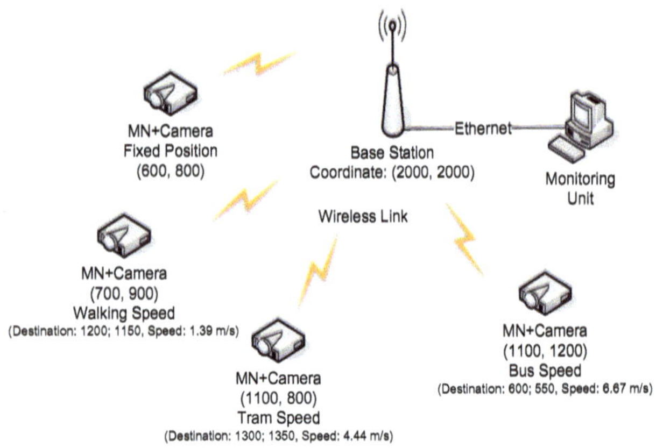

Fig. 3 Simulation configuration

To examine the trade-off on TCP streams between embedded TPP in WiMAX MAC and transport layers, the following scenarios were performed. First, impact of the embedded TPP and ordinary TPP implementations in MAC layer to traffic performances was assessed in term of delay and security coverage. Afterward, the impact of the embedded TPP implementations on transport layer is examined. Finally, both methods were examined for multilink connections by modifying the simulated network.

4 Simulation Results

Figure 4 depicts delay characteristic for various traffic rates when non-embedded (so called normal) TPP over WiMAX and the embedded TPP schemas over WiMAX were applied. The traffics (TCP streams) performance increases significantly when the TPP messages embedded into WiMAX MAC headers. It reduces average delay of TCP streams significantly about 38.4%. The separated TPP message in MAC layer imposes higher delay as number of WiMAX frames increases.

In term of security, all WiMAX signals (Suherman and Mubarakah 2018) are protected in both methods. Besides sending TCP streams, SS and BS also exchange other WiMAX signals such as ranging request/response, MAC initialization, MAC arrangement, DL-MAP processing, DCD processing, UCD processing, registration, mobile neighbor advertisement, fast power control, authorization-invalid and reset command messages. These signals can be protected as well (Table 1).

Figure 5 shows performance comparisons of the embedded TPP in TCP header and normal TPP sent by using TCP. Normal TPP in Fig. 5 is different from normal TPP in Fig. 4. In Fig. 4, normal TPP messages are sent by using WiMAX frame, while in Fig. 5, normal TPP messages are sent by using TCP payload which means WiMAX frames are not aware of them. Embedded TPP in TCP header successfully decrease TCP streams delay performance significantly about 59.89%. Normal TPP message in TCP flow results higher delay.

In terms of security, the TPP implementation in transport layer is only able to protect TCP streams only. WiMAX link will have greater risk as depicted in Table 2.

By comparing simulation results in Figs. 4 and 5, embedded TPP in MAC layer exerts 18.4 ms higher delay in average. This higher delay is due to more encryption processes in MAC layer than in transport layer. This delay is still low enough for real-time applications. However, delay may increase in multiple link connections. In security view, embedded TPP in MAC layer provides better link protection than the second method since all other WiMAX signals are protected. In case existing WiMAX link protection within

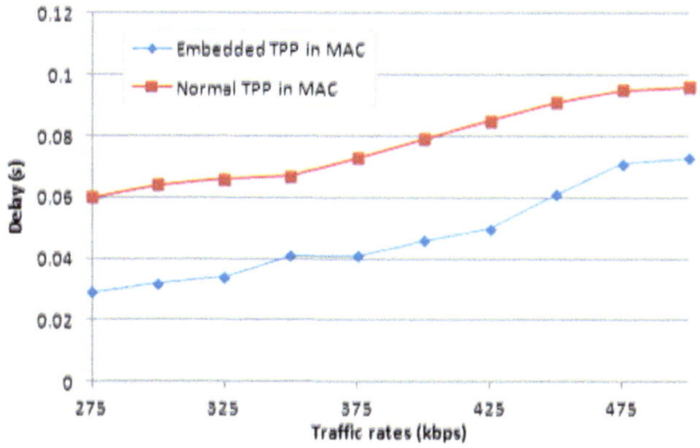

Fig. 4 TCP stream performances for embedded TPP in MAC layer

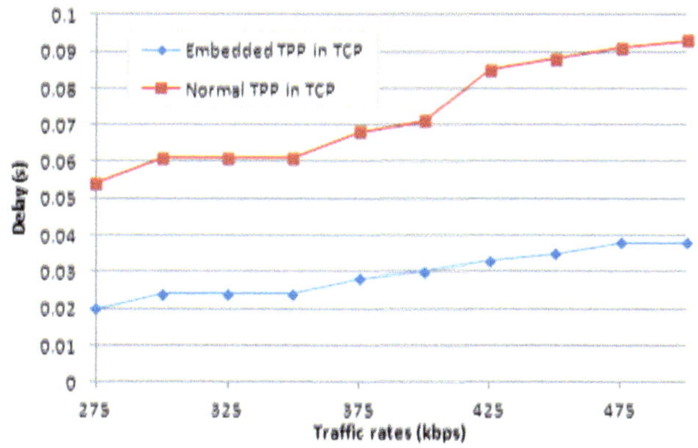

Fig. 5 TCP stream performances for embedded TPP in transport layer

Table 1 Security protection comparisons for embedded TPP in MAC layer

WiMAX signal	Protection			
	Embedded TPP	Normal TPP	No TPP	Non-protection risks
TCP streams	Yes	Yes	No	Water torture, DoS
Ranging request/Response	Yes	Yes	No	Water torture, DoS
MAC initialization	Yes	Yes	No	Masquerading, DoS
MAC arrangement	Yes	Yes	No	Masquerading, DoS
DL-MAP processing	Yes	Yes	No	Scrambling, DoS
DCD processing	Yes	Yes	No	Scrambling, DoS
UCD processing	Yes	Yes	No	Scrambling, DoS
Registration	Yes	Yes	No	Masquerading, DoS
Neighbor advertise	Yes	Yes	No	Water torture, DoS
Fast power control	Yes	Yes	No	Water torture, DoS
Authorization-invalid	Yes	Yes	No	Masquerading, DoS
Reset command	Yes	Yes	No	Water torture, DoS

Table 2 Security protection comparisons for embedded TPP in transport layer

WiMAX signal	Protection			
	Embedded TPP	TPP	No TPP	Non-protection risks
TCP streams	Yes	Yes	No	Water torture, DoS
Ranging request/Response	No	No	No	Water torture, DoS
MAC initialization	No	No	No	Masquerading, DoS
MAC arrangement	No	No	No	Masquerading, DoS
DL-MAP processing	No	No	No	Scrambling, DoS
DCD processing	No	No	No	Scrambling, DoS
UCD processing	No	No	No	Scrambling, DoS
Registration	No	No	No	Masquerading, DoS
Neighbor advertise	No	No	No	Water torture, DoS
Fast power control	No	No	No	Water torture, DoS
Authorization-invalid	No	No	No	Masquerading, DoS
Reset command	No	No	No	Water torture, DoS

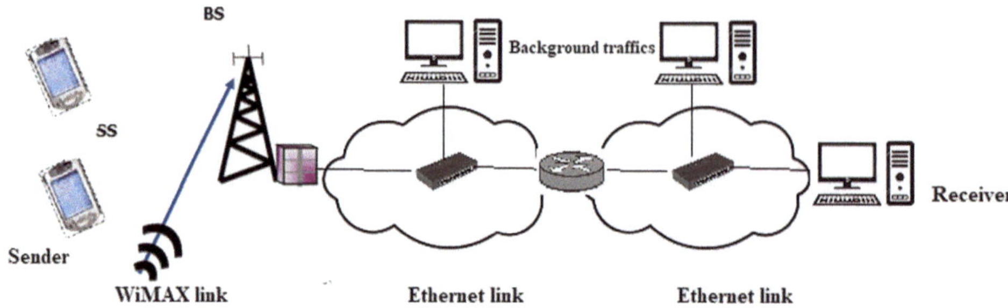

Fig. 6 Multiple link simulation

Table 3 Security protection in multiple links

Signal	Embedded TPP in WiMAX MAC header		Embedded TPP in TCP header	
	WiMAX link	Other links	WiMAX link	Other links
TCP streams	Yes	No	Yes	Yes
Other signals	Yes	No	No	No

the standard is secure enough, embedded TPP in TCP layer is preferred as TCP streams experienced best performances.

Additional assessment on multiple links as shown in Fig. 6 produces insignificant delay difference between embedded TPP in WiMAX MAC header and embedded TPP in transport layer. Both methods produced average stream delay 57.6 ms and 57.2 ms subsequently. The embedded TPP in transport layer protects TCP streams end to end, both WiMAX and other links, while embedded TPP in WiMAX MAC layer protects TCP streams in WiMAX link only as written in Table 3.

5 Conclusions

This paper has examined embedded TPP into MAC header and embedded TPP into TCP header to provide secured TCP streams. Embedding TPP messages into WiMAX header results 62.59% higher delay than embedding TPP into TCP header. However, the first method protects all WiMAX signals, while the latter only protect TCP streams. Attack on WiMAX signals such as ranging and MAC arrangement may cause TCP streams compromised.

In multilink connections, embedding TPP on MAC header protects TCP streams in WiMAX link but not in other links. On the other hand, embedded TPP in TCP header is able to provide end to end protection, which means TCP flows in all links are secured. The method also exerts a slightly lower delay (0.7%) than embedding in MAC header. Future work may explore embedded TPP integration to existing security protocols.

References

Ahson, S.A., and M. Ilyas (eds.). 2018. *WiMAX: Standards and security*. CRC Press.

Al-Akaidi, M., R. Hamzaoui, and Suherman. 2012. Transport and MAC cross-layer protocol for video surveillance over WIMAX. Eurosis.

Alezabi, K.A., F. Hashim, S.J. Hashim, B.M. Ali, and A. Jamalipour. 2016. Authentication process enhancements in WiMAX networks. *Security and Communication Networks* 9 (17): 4703–4725.

Anbazhagan, R., and N. Rangaswamy. 2013. Contention resolution with EIED backoff for bandwidth request in IEEE 802.16 networks. *AEU-International Journal of Electronics and Communications* 67(1): 40–44.

Badawi, A., and M. Zarlis. 2019. Impact three pass protocol modifications to key transmission performance. *Journal of Physics: Conference Series* 1235 (1): 012050.

Chen, L.W., Y.C. Tseng. 2008. Design and analysis of contention-based request schemes for best-effort traffics in IEEE 802.16 networks. *IEEE Communications Letters* 12(8): 602–604.

IEEE Std. 802.16-2004. Local and Metropolitan Area Networks, Part 16: Air Interface for Fixed Broadband Wireless Access Systems, IEEE, Oct 2004.

IEEE Std. 802.16e-2005. Local and Metropolitan Area Networks, Part 16: Air Interface for Fixed and Mobile Broadband Wireless Access Systems, Dec 2005.

IEEE Std 802.16m-2011. Local and metropolitan area networks Part 16: Air Interface for Broadband Wireless Access Systems, 1–1112. IEEE, 5 May 2011.

Kumar, C., Y. Arya, and G. Agarwal. 2018. A review report on WiMAX vulnerabilities, security threats and their solutions. In *Second International Conference on Inventive Communication and Computational Technologies (ICICCT)*, 1963–1967.

Lakshmi, T.S.S. 2017. SoC implementation of AES 128 bit algorithm for IEEE 802.16 e mobile WiMax standards. CVR Journal of Science and Technology 13(1): 16–20.

Mubarakah, N., M.Y. Al-Hakim, and E. Warman. 2018. Energy consumption model on WiMAX subscriber station. In *IOP Conference Series: Materials Science and Engineering* 309(1): 012002.

Oguta, S.O. 2018. Enhancing Security of Wimax Communication System Using Diffie Hellman Algorithm, JKUAT-COETEC.

Panda, P.K., and S. Chattopadhyay. 2019. A modified PKM environment for the security enhancement of IEEE 802.16 e. *Computer Standards & Interfaces* 61: 107–120.

Sangwan, A., and V.R. Singh. 2017. A secure authentication scheme for WiMax network and verification using scyther tool. *International Journal of Applied Engineering Research* 12 (11): 3002–3008.

Simion, D., M.F. Ursuleanu, and A. Graur. 2012. An overview on WiMAX security weaknesses/potential solutions. In *Proceedings 11th International Conference on Development and Application Systems, Suceava, Romania*, 98–102.

Suherman, S., and M. Al–Akaidi. 2014. An efficient negative acknowledgement–based transport protocol in 802.11 media streaming. *International Journal of Ad Hoc and Ubiquitous Computing* 16(3): 161–171.

Suherman, S., and N. Mubarakah. 2018. State and duration model of energy consumption in a Wimax mobile device. *International Journal of Engineering & Technology* 7(3.2): 2008.

Suherman, S., N. Mubarakah, and M. Al-Akaidi. 2015. A transport layer protocol for uplink WiMAX video streaming. *International Journal of Multimedia & Ubiquitous Engineering* 10 (1): 19–32.

Suherman, Deddy Dikmawanto, Syafruddin Hasan. 2020. Embedding the three pass protocol messages into transmission control protocol header. *International Journal of Electrical Engineering and Computer Science* (in press).

Thapa, A., and S. Shin. 2009. Utility based backoff (UBB) algorithm for initial ranging procedure in WiBro. In *Proceedings of IEEE 69th VTC*, 1–5.

Tian, Y., K. Xu, and N. Ansari. 2005. TCP in wireless environments: Problems and solutions. *IEEE Communications Magazine* 43 (3): S27–S32.

Vu, H.L., S. Chan, and L. Andrew. 2010. Performance Analysis of Best-Effort Service in Saturated IEEE 802.16 Networks. IEEE Transactions on Vehicular Technology 59(1): 460–472.

Xiong, G., S. Han, Y. Zhang, Y. Zhu, J.K. Fwu. 2020. U.S. Patent No. 10,555,322. Washington, DC: U.S. Patent and Trademark Office.

Yadav, K., L. Ratusaria, D. Swaroop, and B. Kumar. 2018. Computationally efficient WiMax with handover scheme using Elliptic Curve Diffie Hellman (ECDH) Key Agreement Protocol. In *2018 International Conference on Computing, Power and Communication Technologies (GUCON)*, 831–836. IEEE.

An Empirical Analysis of Machine Learning Efficacy in Anti-Ransomware Tools

Hiba Zuhair and Ali Selamat

Abstract

Researchers attempt to develop more competent anti-ransomware tools that assisted by machine learning classifiers to mitigate the threats of ransomware, protect the privacy of cyber users, and survive the security of cyberspace. However, their achievements remain insufficient in their efficacy against zero-day variants and/or imperviously detected families of ransomware during real-time practice. This is due to their partial characterizing sets of traits, limited analysis of static and dynamic actions, lacking the semi-realistic testbeds, heavy use of computer footprints, indecisive classification margins, and unavailability of representative datasets, inactive learning mechanisms. To emphasize the causality between their contributions and shortages, this paper analyzes the applied machine learning classifier in the existing anti-ransomware tools empirically. Also, it qualifies their attributes and shortages to affirm their efficacy and sufficiency for real-time ransomware detection. Empirical outcomes yield notable facets to study in the future work that will boost up the current achievements in the anti-ransomware domain.

Keywords

Crypto-ransomware · Locker-ransomware · Static analysis · Dynamic analysis · Machine learning

H. Zuhair (✉)
Department of Systems Engineering, College of Information Engineering, Al-Nahrain University, Baghdad, Iraq
e-mail: hiba.zuhir@coie-nahrain.edu.iq; hiba.zuhair.pcs2013@gmail.com

A. Selamat
Malaysia Japan International Institute of Technology (MJIIT), Universiti Teknologi Malaysia, Kuala Lumpur, Malaysia
e-mail: aselamat@utm.my

1 Introduction

Motivating by the fame and the illegal profit, the cybercriminals have threatened the users' privacy and their information systems' protection by ransomware attacks (Bhardwaj et al. 2016). Thus, many achievements have been done during the last decade in academia and industry to mitigate ransomware consequences effectively (Bhardwaj et al. 2016; Richardson and North 2017). Different anti-ransomware tools and apps have been developed to detect zero-day ransomware variants of various ransomware families on windows and portable platforms (Bhardwaj et al. 2016; Richardson and North 2017). Along with them are those relied on machine learning classifiers that employ a set of static traits and/or dynamic actions to examine a ransomware attack at its runtime successfully (Bhardwaj et al. 2016; Richardson and North 2017; Al-rimy et al. 2018; Tailor and Patel 2017). However, those most proficient tools still suffer from late ransomware tackle, somewhat faulty ransomware family categorization among other malware families. Besides they performed differently, they achieved complex computations with heavy use of CPU and memory space during a long elapsed time (Al-rimy et al. 2018; Kok et al. 2019; Zavarsky and Lindskog 2016). Such heavy-weight anti-ransomware tools provided more chances to cybercriminals who would bypass them by their own zero-day and/or zero-hour variants. Thus, the cybercriminals still able to exploit adversarial traits in new families of ransomware and defeat the existing ransomware defense schemes. Then, more data loss, data leakage, money losses would be produced along with other tragic concerns to the cybersecurity (Al-rimy et al. 2018; Tailor and Patel 2017; Kok et al. 2019; Zavarsky and Lindskog 2016). However, researchers' efforts are never-ending to develop more proficient anti-ransomware tools toward an optimal user's data privacy, users' system protection, and then a safe cyberspace (Kharraz and Kirda 2017; Kharaz et al. 2016; Morato et al. 2018; Gómez-Hernández et al. 2018; Cabaj et al. 2018; Hampton

© The Author(s), under exclusive license to Springer Nature Switzerland AG 2024
A. Salman and A. Tharwat (eds.), *ICT for Engineering & Critical Infrastructures*,
Advances in Science, Technology & Innovation, https://doi.org/10.1007/978-3-031-49309-6_6

et al. 2018; Feng et al. 2017; Alhawi et al. 2018; Sgandurra et al. 2016; Continella et al. 2016; Bae et al. 2020; Shaukat and Ribeiro 2018; Zuhair and Selamat 2019a, b; Malware Black List; virustotal). For this purpose, this paper studies the existing anti-ransomware tools that assisted by machine learning classifiers in an empirical context. It critically qualifies the existing anti-ransomware tools in terms of their machine leaners, sets of traits, types of traits, and the families of ransomware that they could recognize. Furthermore, it affirms their qualification by justifying their detection capabilities empirically across scalable and variable datasets. Then, the empirical outputs address the causality between the classifiers' performance and their limitations that could restate what issues were overlooked by the existing anti-ransomware tools and how they should be enriched in future works. To attain the aforesaid goals, the remaining of this paper is organized as follows: Sect. 2 presents ransomware families and surveys the most recently published works that applied machine learning classifiers, whereas Sect. 3 analyzes the applied machine learning classifiers empirically to highlight their limitations and restate their best future outlook. At last, Sect. 4 concludes the overall investigated facets in this paper.

2 Literature Survey

Typically, a ransomware variant is a kind of malicious pattern aiming at either blocking the victim's computer system or encrypting the victim's data and then demanding a ransom payment from the victim to recover his/her system or decrypt his/her own data (Bhardwaj et al. 2016; Richardson and North 2017; Al-rimy et al. 2018; Tailor and Patel 2017; Kok et al. 2019; Zavarsky and Lindskog 2016). To deceive the users and intrude on their computer systems, cybercriminals pursue a "recipe-to-success" strategy. First, the victim catches the bait via an email attachment or spoofed link that is under the cybercriminal control. Then, cybercriminal disseminates the ransomware variant through the vulnerabilities of the victim's computer system to infect system's settings, file locations, and system directories. Crypto-ransomware variant encrypts particular victim's files and halts the infected system, whereas locker-ransomware targets a particular system's files and their locations to disable the victim's access and halts the system. Accordingly, the ransomware variant activates the user's notification to acquire a ransom for either decrypting the victim's files or unblocks the user's access to the system (Al-rimy et al. 2018; Tailor and Patel 2017; Kok et al. 2019; Zavarsky and Lindskog 2016). As time progresses, cybercriminals emerge from various families of crypto and locker ransomware that exploiting many variants. Crypto- and locker-ransomware families and variants are rapidly increased, advanced, and disseminated to infect computer systems of different platforms like Microsoft Windows. To do so, ransomware variants run sophisticated intrusion methods, more potential encryption techniques, and maneuvering software applications (Zavarsky and Lindskog 2016; Kharraz and Kirda 2017; Kharaz et al. 2016; Morato et al. 2018; Gómez-Hernández et al. 2018; Cabaj et al. 2018; Hampton et al. 2018; Feng et al. 2017; Alhawi et al. 2018). Examples of crypto- and locker-ransomware families are described briefly in Table 1.

To thwart ransomware families and their own variants during the last decade, researchers have developed various anti-ransomware tools that assisted by misuse and anomaly detection schemes. Misuse detection schemes have adopted static ransomware analysis, where-as, anomaly detection schemes have deployed dynamic ransomware analysis (Bhardwaj et al. 2016; Richardson and North 2017; Al-rimy et al. 2018; Tailor and Patel 2017; Kok et al. 2019; Zavarsky and Lindskog 2016). In spite of their effective detection versus the generic ransomware families, they have produced high false detections and mis-detections versus ransomware variants and newly emerged ransomware families in real-time application (Al-rimy et al. 2018; Tailor and Patel 2017; Kok et al. 2019; Zavarsky and Lindskog 2016). This is due to inspect the static traits of ransomware variants rather than their dynamic actions, or tracing the dynamic behaviors of ransomware variants exclusively (Zavarsky and Lindskog 2016; Kharraz and Kirda 2017; Kharaz et al. 2016; Morato et al. 2018; Gómez-Hernández et al. 2018; Cabaj et al. 2018; Hampton et al. 2018; Feng et al. 2017). Thus, they have performed differently against zero-day ransomware variants and all-inclusive ransomware families. Also, they have been circumvented by more sophisticated actions of the newly emerged ransomware families (Zavarsky and Lindskog 2016; Kharraz and Kirda 2017; Kharaz et al. 2016; Morato et al. 2018; Gómez-Hernández et al. 2018; Cabaj et al. 2018; Hampton et al. 2018; Feng et al. 2017; Alhawi et al. 2018). Due to their limited efficacy in a real-time application, the recent works have leveraged machine learning classifiers to discriminate ransomware families and their own variants from those of good-ware apps and other malware families effectively and efficiently (Richardson and North 2017; Al-rimy et al. 2018; Alhawi et al. 2018). Examples of these works assisted by machine learning classifiers are described briefly in Table 2.

3 Emirical Analysis and Discussion

For the empirical analysis, standard evaluation measurements were used to qualify the empirical results, for example, true-positive rate (TPR), false-positive rate (FPR), and

Table 1 Windows platform-based ransomware attacks (Zavarsky and Lindskog 2016; Kharraz and Kirda 2017; Kharaz et al. 2016; Morato et al. 2018; Gómez-Hernández et al. 2018; Cabaj et al. 2018; Hampton et al. 2018; Feng et al. 2017; Alhawi et al. 2018)

Ransomware family	Year	Type	Infection strategy	Damage (s)
AiDS	1989	Crypto	It was delivered to computer-based information systems via floppy disks	• Leakage of root directories • Loss of system files
GpCode	2005	Crypto	It was developed with a symmetric encryption algorithm to encrypt users' data files	• Holding up the banking information systems • Loss of system and user files
Archiveus	2006	Crypto	It was applied with RSA algorithm to encrypt system files	• Ruining the original version of windows platform • Data loss • Money loss
WinLock	2008	Locker	It locked the computer system and demanding ransom via sending SMS to victim's phone number	• Holding up the operating system • Loss of backup data • Loss of money
Reveton	2012	Locker	It impersonated the law enforcement agencies to deceive users with rumor claims	• Holding up the operating system • Abusing the prepaid electronic payment platforms • Loss of backup data
Crypto-locker	2013	Crypto	It encrypted the file's contents by RSA algorithm with private and public keys	• The halt of targeting system • Loss of backup data • Loss of money
Crypto-wall	2014	Crypto	It encrypted the system files and injected malicious codes which freezes the system's firewalls	• Leakage of original system files • Loss of user files • Loss of money in bitcoins
Ransom as service (RaaS)	2015	Locker	It used the social engineering techniques to impersonate a good-ware website as a malicious website in the dark web	• The halt of targeting systems • Loss of backup data • Loss of money in bitcoins
Cerber	2016	Crypto	It injected the malicious instructions to overwrite an encrypted content onto the original system	• Loss of original system files • Deactivation of the system registry
Crysis	2016	Crypto	It encrypted the system files, rewrote their contents, and renamed them	• Leakage of system files • Loss of user data • Loss of backup data
Locky	2016	Locker	It used the social engineering techniques to intrude the system through vulnerabilities of system settings, deactivated the registry actions, and removed the backup data	• The halt of targeting system • Loss of backup data • Money loss
Wanna cry	2017	Crypto	It encrypted the contents of the system files and removed the original system files	• Data loss • Holding up the operating system • Money loss in bitcoins
Sopra	2017	Crypto	It encrypted the contents of the system files and removed the original system files	• Data loss • Holding up the operating system • Money loss in bitcoins
Zeus	2018	Crypto	It encrypted the contents of systems files and created new files with extensions belonging to different ransomware versions	• The halt targeting system of industrial organization • Backup data loss • Money loss

false-negative rate (FNR) (Sgandurra et al. 2016; Continella et al. 2016; Bae et al. 2020; Shaukat and Ribeiro 2018; Zuhair and Selamat 2019a, b). Furthermore, the scores of AUC are used to quantify how often did the comparable machine learning classifiers take to detect zero-day ransomware variants and categorize their corresponding ransomware families during real-time practice. As shown in Fig. 1, six machine learning classifiers were testified and qualified on a dataset of 35,000 ransomware variants belonging to 14 topmost families of both crypto and locker types that were collected from publically used malware data archives (Malware Black List; virustotal; virusshare; contagiodump). In addition, 500 good-ware instances of trustworthy apps were collected and were aggregated for eight months (from 1/1/2019 to 1/9/2019). Dataset was formulated into vectors of traits according to a hybrid set of 24 static and dynamic traits that typically adopted by the related works as they presented in Table 3. Then, the vectors of traits were randomly partitioned into 2/3nd and 1/3rd vectors as training and testing datasets, respectively. The training dataset was used to learn the machine learning classifiers and generate the threat class models, whereas the testing dataset was used to testify the threat class models and obtain the detection outputs (see Fig. 1).

The empirical results, as they are presented in Figs. 2 and 3, manifested the detection capabilities of the six comparable machine learning classifiers against zero-day ransomware variants and their corresponding families. In Fig. 2a, HMLC, DT, and NB performed significant TPRs, FPRs, and FNRs versus ransomware variants among its competitors across the training and testing datasets. This was because of their ability to learn large and hybrid sets of both static and dynamic traits. Indeed, this hybrid set of traits provided an optimal configuration of traits' variety and quantity. Thus, the aforesaid classifiers could characterize ransomware actions holistically. While their competitors achieved insignificant TPRs, FPRs, and FNRs because of their inadaptability to characterize a big and hybrid set of 24 ransomware traits. Definitely, this variation of efficacy demonstrated how the hybrid set of static and dynamic traits was a significant factor of holistic ransomware characterization. The discriminating power of the hybrid set of traits was rich enough to characterize a ransomware variant among other suspicious and good-ware variants in the dataset.

On the other hand, the classifiers of high TPRs and low FPRs showed that they could decisively categorize a particular ransomware family among other families that might share the same traits, see Fig. 2a and b. Precisely, a set of generic and decisive traits could be a crucial factor to categorize ransomware families successfully. This revealed the need to select the best set of traits for ransomware family's categorization along with on a class imbalanced dataset. In addition, the dataset size and the dataset aggregation time (i.e., the age of aggregated datasets) had a negative influence on detecting the variants of 14 ransomware families that were imbalanced across the training and testing datasets; see Fig. 2a, b and c. Because the utilized datasets were comprised of 14 passive variants along with the active variants of ransomware families; the classifiers generated default threat models by learning the training datasets. The default threat models were unadaptable to detect any never seen ransomware variant included in the testing dataset.

So far, the plotted results in Fig. 3 showed that almost comparable classifiers achieved approximately high-to-moderate scores of AUC at classifying zero-day ransomware variants during 30 days of real-time analysis (from November 1 to November 30, 2019). This was related to the scalability and variety of the real-world dataset that was investigated during the real-time analysis. Such a dataset might contain the daily emerged variants of all ransomware, malware, and good-ware families. Altogether, they required regulated decisive functions, probably pruning factors, and multi-class induction settings to adapt them. Furthermore, they needed changeable time, computations, and computer footprints to characterize every sample and to classify its probable case of multi-class effectively. So far, any suspicious variant might be neither truly classified as ransomware, nor truly classified as good-ware, nor truly classified as malware app accurately. That, in turn, might decrease the efficacy of ransomware machine learning classifier and its robustness versus imbalanced, scalable, and multi-class dataset.

4 Issues and Perspectives

The aforesaid findings referred to some outstanding issues that the competitive classifiers overlooked, and how such issues should be outlooked in the future. First issue, the six comparable machine learning classifiers fall short in classifying almost traits of the prevalent ransomware families. This was attributed to their generic analysis of either static traits or dynamic traits among 24 various traits that all were exploited by 14 ransomware families exclusively. Thus, they were unable to characterize such a big and a hybrid set of 24 static and dynamic traits holistically. That, in turn, became insignificant factor which reduced their decisive classification against many variants of 14 ransomware families among other suspicious and good-ware variants in training/testing dataset.

Second issue, they were incompetent to tracking the dynamic actions of ransomware families because they lacked the semi-realistic testbed which must be pursued under realistic conditions similar the real-time environment. Such semi-realistic testbed could provide a trigger to different ransomware payloads, linking libraries, and enable particular access permissions. Third issue, the decisive boundaries of the classifiers were default to distinguish the traits of a new ransomware family among these of prevalent ransomware families and good-ware applications as well as other malware families. Thus, they performed differently on an imbalanced dataset of multi-family variants (ransomware, good-ware, and malware families). Accordingly, the empirical dataset was a sub-optimally representative dataset to detect ransomware variants that probably shared similar traits, functionalities, and exploitations with malware variants.

Since the synthesis of ransomware variants was carried out on a dataset collected as batches of variants at different time to be include in the empirical datasets, the comparable machine learning classifiers were unadaptable to classify zero-day ransomware variants. This was because their decisive boundaries were not ultimately tuned to generate the ideal threat model during real-time practice that is the fourth outstanding issue.

Table 2 Recent related works that applied machine learning-based ransomware detection

Related work	Method	Classifier	Limitations
Sgandurra et al. (2016)	It detected the updates of API calls, registry key and file system operations via a sandbox versus locker-ransomware families	LR, NB, SVM	• Exclusive for locker ransomware • Unaware of static ransomware analysis • Unaware of multi-class detection • Unaware of zero-day variants • Unaware of real-time detection • Computer footprints • Time-sensitive with high false-positive rates
Continella et al. (2016)	It detected some crypto-ransomware families that exploit generic ransomware traits like I/O and low-level file system infections, encrypting file contents, and overwriting the original contents by monitoring file system activity and then updating the threat profile overtime on a realistic environment	DT	• Exclusive for crypto-ransomware • Unaware multi-class detection • Heavy use of computer footprints • Time-sensitive with high false-positive rates • Original data loss or leakage
Bae et al. (2020)	It used dynamic traits and six machine learning algorithms to detect zero-day variants of locker-ransomware versions among malware and good-ware apps	DT LR BN	• Exclusive for locker ransomware • Unaware of real-time detection • Original data leakage or loss • No static traits analysis • Varied performance outcomes
Shaukat and Ribeiro (2018)	A multi-layered tool detected zero-day variants of crypto-ransomware families by developing a generalized model comprises static and dynamic traits	LR SVM NN RF	• Exclusive for crypto ransomware • Unaware of multi-class detection • Unaware of real-time detection • Time-sensitive with high false-positive rates • Ensemble classifier design is needed for the best decision-making function
Zuhair and Selamat (2019a, b)	A hybrid machine learning-based and multi-tier anti-ransomware tool that detected zero-day variants of both crypto- and locker-ransomware families by using dynamic traits on windows platform in real-time application	HMLC	• Unaware of static analysis • Exclusive to seven families of crypto- and locker-ransomware variants • Unaware of multi-class detection

Notes DT, LR, BN, NN, NB, SVM, and HMLC refer to Decision Tree, Logistic Regression, Bayesian Network, Neural Network, Naïve Bayes, Random Forest, Support Vector Machine, and Hybrid Machine Learning Classifier

Fig. 1 Empirical workflow

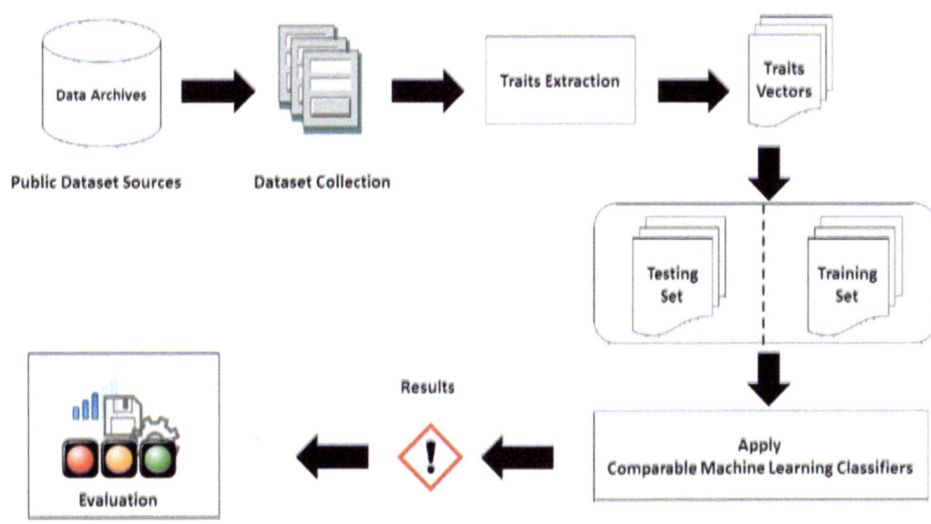

Precisely, several facets were overlooked in the literature of anti-ransomware tools that assisted by machine learning classifiers as presented in Table 4. To outlook these facets in the future, more efficacious machine learning classifier must be applied for real-time and zero-day ransomware detection. They are: (i) deployment of adversary traits that

Table 3 Hybrid set of ransomware traits

Traits	Type	"Ransomware families"													
		Crypto-Wall	Win-Lock	Reventon	Crypto-Locker	Archiveus	GpCode	AiDS	RaaS	Cerber	Locky	Crysis	Wanna-Cry	Sopra	Zeus
"Windows API calls"	Dynamic	✖	✓	✓		✖	✖	✖	✖	✖	✓	✖	✖	✖	✖
"Windows cryptographic APIs"	Dynamic	✓	✖	✓	✓	✓	✓	✖	✖	✓	✖	✓	✖	✓	✖
"Registry key"	Dynamic	✓	✖	✓	✓	✖	✖	✖	✖	✖	✓	✖	✖	✖	✖
"System file process"	Dynamic	✓	✖	✖	✓	✖	✖	✖	✓	✓	✓	✓	✖	✖	✖
"Directory actions"	Dynamic	✓	✓	✖	✓	✖	✖	✖	✖	✖	✖	✓	✓	✓	✓
"Application folders"	Dynamic	✓	✓	✖	✓	✖	✖	✖	✖	✖	✓	✓	✓	✓	✓
"Control panel settings"	Dynamic	✓	✖	✓	✓	✖	✖	✖	✖	✖	✓	✖	✓	✖	✓
"System file locations"	Dynamic	✓	✖	✖	✓	✖	✖	✖	✓	✓	✓	✓	✖	✖	✖
"Pay-loaders/Downloaders"	Dynamic	✓	✖	✓	✓	✖	✖	✖	✖	✖	✓	✖	✓	✖	✓
"Command and control server"	Dynamic	✓	✓	✓	✓	✖	✖	✖	✓	✖	✓	✖	✓	✖	✓
"Windows volume shadow (vssadmin.exe andWMIC. exe)"	Dynamic	✖	✓	✓	✖	✖	✖	✖	✓	✖	✓	✖	✓	✖	✓
"File fingerprint"	Dynamic	✓	✖	✖	✓	✖	✓	✖	✖	✓	✖	✓	✖	✖	✖
"Directory listing queries"	Dynamic	✓	✖	✖	✓	✖	✖	✖	✓	✓	✓	✓	✖	✖	✖
"Windows safe mode booting (bcdedit.exe)"	Dynamic	✖	✓	✓	✖	✖	✖	✓	✓	✖	✓	✖	✓	✓	✓
"File extensions"	Static	✓	✓	✓	✓	✓	✓	✖	✖	✓	✖	✓	✓	✓	✓
"Files names"	Static	✖	✖	✖	✖	✓	✖	✓	✖	✓	✖	✓	✓	✓	✓
"Portable executable header"	Static	✖	✓	✓	✖	✖	✖	✓	✓	✖	✓	✖	✓	✓	✓
"Embedded resources"	Static	✖	✓	✓	✖	✖	✖	✓	✓	✖	✓	✖	✓	✓	✓
"Packers"	Static	✖	✓	✓	✖	✖	✖	✓	✓	✖	✓	✖	✓	✓	✓
"Shannon's entropy"	Static	✓	✖	✓	✓	✓	✓	✖	✖	✓	✖	✖	✖	✖	✖
"Cryptors"	Static	✓	✖	✓	✓	✓	✓	✖	✖	✓	✖	✖	✖	✖	✖
"Portable executable signature"	Static	✖	✓	✓	✖	✖	✖	✓	✓	✖	✓	✖	✓	✓	✓
"Embedded scripts"	Static	✖	✓	✓	✖	✖	✖	✓	✓	✖	✓	✖	✓	✓	✓
"Fuzzy hashing"	Static	✓	✖	✓	✓	✓	✓	✖	✖	✓	✖	✖	✓	✖	✖

Fig. 2 Efficacy of the comparable machine learning classifiers during empirical analysis

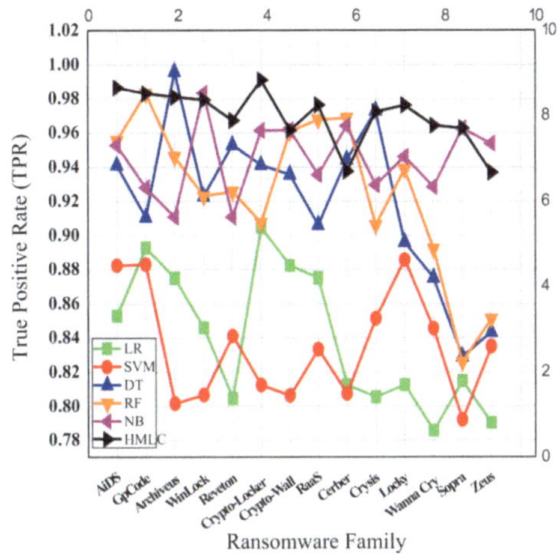

(a) TPR vs. 14 Ransomware Families

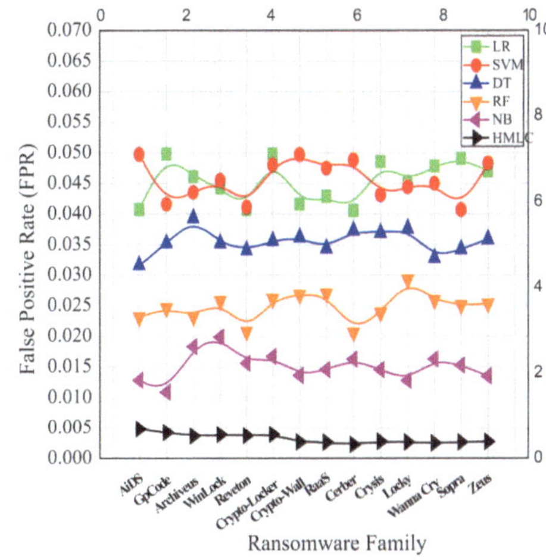

(b) FPR vs. 14 Ransomware Families

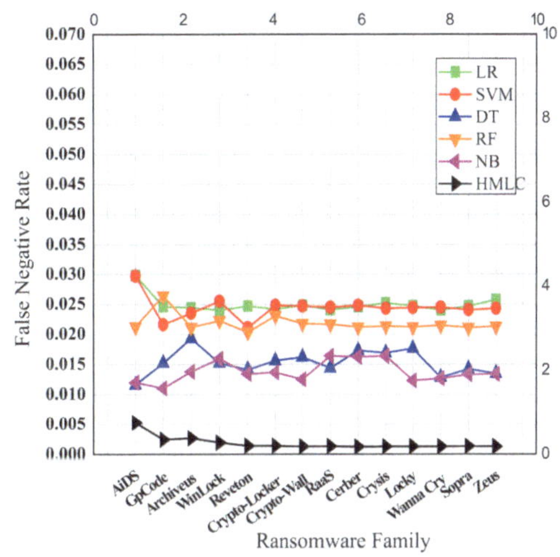

(c) FNR vs. Ransomware Families

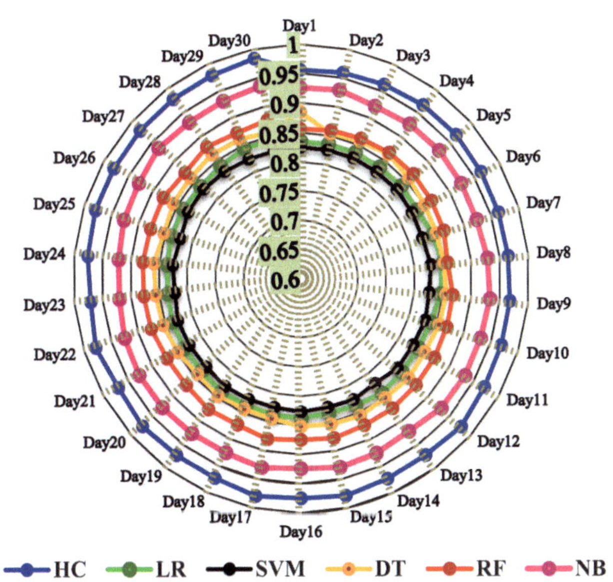

Fig. 3 Efficacy of comparable classifiers during 30 days of realistic analysis

have been exploited by all ransomware families for holistic ransomware characterization, (ii) the best traits set selection that would promote the decision margins of machine learning classifier for decisive ransomware classification among other malware apps, (iii) actively learned classifier with ultimately adjustment of its decisive margins for zero-day ransomware classification in real-time practice, (iv) hybrid classifier would tune, prune, and synchronize the decisive margins of multi- and complementary machine learning classifiers better than single and ensemble classifiers for adaptive ransomware detection versus big and imbalanced dataset, and (v) the use of semi-realistic testbed would customize the overall efficacy of the classifier and control the trade-off between ransomware streaming analysis and computer footprints (i.e., CPU and memory footprints) during real-time practice.

Table 4 General comparison of related works in ransomware detection

Work / Issues	Sgandurra et al. (2016)	Continella et al. (2016)	Bae et al. (2020)	Shaukat and Ribeiro (2018)	Zuhair and Selamat (2019a, b)
Machine learning classifier	LR, NB, SVM	DT	DT, LR, BN	LR, SVM, NN, RF	HMLC
Type of ransomware traits	Dynamic	Dynamic	Dynamic	Hybrid	Dynamic
Dataset size	1524 samples	2628	2200 samples	996 samples	10,500 samples
Type of detected variants	R, G	R, G	R, M, G	R, G	R, G
Ransomware families	Locker	Crypto	Locker	Crypto	Crypto and locker
Number of tested ransomware families	11 families	11 families	12 families	12 families	7 families
Zero-day ransomware detection	Not	Yes	Yes	Yes	Yes
Testbed of validation	Sandbox	Realistic	Sandbox	Sandbox	Realistic
Real-time validation	Not	Yes	Not	Not	Yes
Type of class detection	Binary-class	Binary-class	Multi-class	Binary-class	Binary-class
♠Performance outcomes	93.3% Detection rate	99.74% TPR 0.27% FPR	98.65% Detection rate	98.25% TPR 0.56% FPR	96.27% Detection rate

Notes DT, LR, BN, NN, NB, SVM, RF, and HMLC refer to Decision Tree, Logistic Regression, Bayesian Network, Neural Network, Naïve Bayes, Random Forest, Support Vector Machine, Random Forest, and Hybrid Machine Learning Classifier
R, M, G refer to Ransomware variants, Malware variants, Good-ware variants
♠ all performance outcomes are retrieved from the related works

5 Conclusions

The tested and qualified machine learning classifiers adopted by the existing anti-ransomware tools affirmed that they were computationally insufficient for holistic aware characterization, novel-aware classification, and multi-class categorization throughout the empirical analysis. Many reasons relied behind their shortages including amount and variety of the extracted traits to characterize, relevant traits between ransomware and malware families, variable discriminating abilities of the traits, limited number of ransomware families to classify, inactive learning of the classifiers, and unregulated decisive margins of the classifiers along with big, imbalanced, and inconsistent dataset to analyze. To overcome the shortages and boost up the efficacy of machine learning classifiers, several facets of future work were recommended to investigate. Accordingly, more competent anti-ransomware tools will be devoted for efficacious and real-time ransomware detection. Altogether, the presented survey, hybrid set of traits, empirical analysis and results, observations and recommendations will navigate the research directions of ransomware detection and protection schemes in the future.

References

Al-rimy, B.A.S., M.A. Maarof, and S.Z.M. Shaid. 2018. Ransomware threat success factors, taxonomy, and countermeasures: A survey and research directions. *Computers and Security* 74: 144–166.

Alhawi, O.M., J. Baldwin, and A. Dehghantanha. 2018. Leveraging machine learning techniques for windows ransomware network traffic detection. In *Cyber Threat Intelligence*, 93–106.

Bae, S.I., G.B. Lee, and E.G. Im. 2020. Ransomware detection using machine learning algorithms. In *Concurrency and Computation: Practice and Experience*, e5422.

Bhardwaj, A., V. Avasthi, H. Sastry, and G.V.B. Subrahmanyam. 2016. Ransomware digital extortion: A rising new age threat. *Indian Journal of Science and Technology* 9 (14): 1–5.

Cabaj, K., M. Gregorczyk, and W. Mazurczyk. 2018. Software-defined networking-based crypto ransomware detection using HTTP traffic characteristics. *Computers and Electrical Engineering* 66: 353–368.

Continella, A., A. Guagnelli, G. Zingaro, G. De Pasquale, A. Barenghi, S. Zanero, and F. Maggi. 2016. ShieldFS: A self-healing, ransomware-aware filesystem. In *Proceedings of the 32nd Annual Conference on Computer Security Applications*, 336–347, ACM.

Feng, Y., C. Liu, and B. Liu. 2017. Poster: A new approach to detecting ransomware with deception. In *38th IEEE Symposium on Security and Privacy*, IEEE.

Gómez-Hernández, J.A., L. Álvarez-González, and P. García-Teodoro. 2018. R-Locker: Thwarting ransomware action through a honey file-based approach. *Computers and Security* 73: 389–398.

Hampton, N., Z. Baig, and S. Zeadally. 2018. Ransomware behavioural analysis on windows platforms. *Journal of Information Security and Applications* 40: 44–51.

Kharraz, A., and E. Kirda. 2017. Redemption: Real-time protection against ransomware at end-hosts. In *International Symposium on Research in Attacks, Intrusions, and Defenses*, 98–119, Cham: Springer.

Kharaz, A., S. Arshad, C. Mulliner, W.K. Roberson, and E. Krida. 2016. Unveil: A large scale, automated approach to detecting ransomware. In *USINEX Security Symposium*, 757–772.

Kok, S., A. Abdullah, N. Jhanjhi, and M. Supramaniam. 2019. Ransomware, threat and detection techniques: A review. *International Journal of Computer Science and Network Security* 19 (2): 136–147.

Malware Analysis and Malware Samples. http://contagiodump.blogspot.tw/.

Malware Black List—Online Repository of Malicious URLs. http://www.malwareblacklist.com.

Morato, D., E. Berrueta, E. Magaña, and M. Izal. 2018. Ransomware early detection by the analysis of file sharing traffic. *Journal of Network and Computer Applications* 124: 14–32.

Richardson, R., and M. North. 2017. Ransomware: Evolution, mitigation and prevention. *International Management Review* 13 (1): 10–21.

Sgandurra, D., L. Muñoz-González, R. Mohsen, and E.C. Lupu. 2016. Automated dynamic analysis of ransomware: Benefits, limitations and use for detection.

Shaukat, S.K., and V.J. Ribeiro. 2018. RansomWall: A layered defense system against cryptographic ransomware attacks using machine learning. In *2018 10th International Conference on Communication Systems and Networks (COMSNETS)*, 356–363, IEEE.

Tailor, J.P., and A.D. Patel. 2017. A comprehensive survey: Ransomware attacks prevention, monitoring and damage control. *International Journal of Research, Science and Innovation* 4: 2321–2705.

Virus Share. Malware Repository. https://virusshare.com.

Virus Total-Intelligence Search Engine, "Free Online Virus, Malware URL Scanner". https://www.virustotal.com.

Zavarsky, P., and D. Lindskog. 2016. Experimental analysis of ransomware on windows and android platforms: Evolution and characterization. *Procedia Computer Science* 94: 465–472.

Zuhair, H., and A. Selamat. 2019a. An intelligent and real-time ransomware detection tool using machine learning algorithm. *Journal of Theoretical and Applied Information Technology* 97 (23): 3448–3461.

Zuhair, H., and A. Selamat. 2019b. RANDS: A machine learning-based anti-ransomware tool. In *Advancing Technology Industrialization through Intelligent Software Methodologies, Tools and Techniques: Proceedings of the 18th International Conference on New Trends in Intelligent Software Methodologies, Tools and Techniques (SoMeT_19)*, 318, IOS Press, 573–587. https://doi.org/10.3233/FAIA190081.

Conceptual Approach for Multimodal Biometrics FPGA-Based Security System

Maciej Szymkowski and Khalid Saeed

Abstract

Increment of cybersecurity became one of the most important problems that researchers have to deal with it. However, simple passwords or smart cards are not appropriate due to their disadvantages—they are easy to forget or lose. The solution for the above-mentioned problem can be biometrics. In this case the human and their traits are the secret key. Nevertheless, it also has one main drawback that is low efficiency in data collection and preprocessing. This disadvantage can be easily removed by the use of FPGA. By this solution, not only can we speed up the processes but also create one fully automated, consistent biometrics system that will be fast and precise. Moreover, this technology can guarantee higher safety for system internal components. Performed analysis has shown that it is clearly possible to create this kind of system for human identity recognition.

Keywords

Biometrics · Safety systems · FPGA · Hardware approach · User identification · Identity validation

1 Introduction

Recently, one of the most significant issues in computer systems and technologies is the answer to the question—how cybersecurity level can be increased? There are multiple ideas how to deal with this problem. One of them uses traditional passwords with some additional signs whereas another tries to recognize a user with smart cards. However, both of these resolutions have one well-known disadvantage. It is easiness of forget (in the case of passwords) or lose (idea connected with smart cards).

So, it should be analyzed whether other options are currently available. None of the users would like to be exposed to the inability to use the system. The most important solution that can be used in these circumstances is biometrics (Bolle et al. 2004; Saeed and Nagashima 2012). It is the science that on the basis of human measurable traits recognize his identity. It means it is clearly impossible to forget or lose the "password" because the user and his traits are the secret key. In the literature one can easily find classification of these features (elprocus) elprocus. There are two main groups—physiological and behavioral. When it comes to the descriptions of them, it can be claimed that the first group consists of traits that are formed at the beginning of human life and remain unchanged until the end of his life (for example: fingerprint, iris, retina) while behavioral ones can be trained and improved during human whole life. In the second group, one can observe: keystroke dynamics, voice, signature.

However, biometrics has one huge disadvantage. Sometimes, specialized sensors and devices are not efficient enough (the time needed to collect the samples is really huge). It means that software for human recognition based on the samples connected with these systems will not be as efficient as it should be. It is connected with the fact that the application will wait until samples will be collected. Moreover, during recognition process, one can observe some steps by which data is preprocessed—sometimes it also takes too much time (with software-based implementations).

The solution for these problems is connected with moving above-mentioned stages to the devices created with FPGA (xilinx). This idea decreases the time needed for data collection and its preprocessing. Moreover, one can

M. Szymkowski (✉) · K. Saeed
Faculty of Computer Science, Białystok University of Technology, Białystok, Poland
e-mail: m.szymkowski@pb.edu.pl

K. Saeed
e-mail: k.saeed@pb.edu.pl

© The Author(s), under exclusive license to Springer Nature Switzerland AG 2024
A. Salman and A. Tharwat (eds.), *ICT for Engineering & Critical Infrastructures*,
Advances in Science, Technology & Innovation, https://doi.org/10.1007/978-3-031-49309-6_7

create one hardware-based solution that will deal with all primary steps of the selected algorithm. What is surprising, FPGA is also used for speeding up data mining processes (Choromański et al. 2019).

This work presents short summary of current state of the art in FPGA-based biometrics systems and propose new hardware-based approach for human identity recognition. It is organized as follows: In the second subchapter, all interesting ideas are described while in the third one the authors present their own idea. In the next sections, conclusions and future work are given.

2 How Others See the Problem

In the literature, one can easily find diversified approaches to FPGA-based biometrics systems. The authors mostly concentrated on two well-known research papers databases that are: IEEE (ieeexplore.ieee) and Springer-Link (Springer). Most of the described solutions were found in these databases.

The first interesting idea was described in Wei et al. (2004). The authors of this work claimed that most of currently implemented algorithms for biometrics recognition are based on statistical methods. One of them is AdaBoost algorithm used for facial recognition. Moreover, in the work one can read that this solution provides high accuracy, however with huge computational complexity for high-resolution or real-time videos. The authors proposed reimplementation of the solution with FPGA. They observed that this implementation accelerated real-time face recognition around 260 times.

Another algorithm was described in Khalil-Hani and Eng (2010). The authors concentrated on finger veins. At the beginning, they claim that one of the most important problems in biometrics algorithms is impossibility to run them in real time environment. The authors created their own solution for samples collection. It is based on infrared LEDs and modified camera. Then they implemented all algorithms on Linux RTOS with traditional programming language. However, all results were generated on FPGA evaluation board on which Linux RTOS was deployed. In the paper, one cannot observe what was the real speedup value. The authors shortly described obtained results.

Interesting approach was also presented in Eng and Khalil-Hani (2009). In the case of this research, the authors proposed to use hand veins for user recognition. Once again, they implemented all algorithms with usage of traditional programming language. Their solution consists of four main blocks: image capturing, image pre-processing, feature extraction and authentication. The authors run their implementations on FPGA evaluation board and Linux RTOS system. Once again, they do not provide any information about speedup as well as they do not implement their algorithms with hardware programming language.

In Van Trieu and Van Cuong (2016) hybrid approach to face recognition with simplified hidden Markov model (HMM) was described. The authors implemented a part of the algorithm on PC and a part on FPGA board. Data was transferred between them with RS232 communication. The PC module was responsible for the whole training process as well as preprocessing part of the recognition algorithm. FPGA board used the data obtained from PC module to recognize a man with hardware-based recognition algorithms. The authors claimed that their approach run only on PC return recognition results in 280 ms while hybrid solution (images were stored on FPGA SRAM memory) in 60 ms. It means that PC+FPGA solution accelerated more than four times the whole process.

The authors of Mohd-Yasin et al. (2004) proposed an approach to iris recognition based on hybrid solution. It means that the whole system is implemented with MATLAB and VHDL. In this algorithm, image processing part was created with MATLAB solution and run on traditional PC while the recognition part based on neural networks (3-layers) was implemented with VHDL on FPGA evaluation board. The authors provided only accuracy results; they do not consider acceleration parameters.

In Pudzs et al. (2013) the authors proposed a novel approach to human recognition on the basis of palmprint and palm veins implemented with FPGA. In this work, the whole solution, starting from image acquisition and ending with final recognition result, was implemented with hardware programming language. Moreover, the authors also provided a specialized module for data encryption (also created with FPGA). In their work, they claimed that the whole recognition process ended after 0.8 s. However, the biggest disadvantage of their work is missing of comparison with software implementation.

The short summary of all described research papers is presented in Table 1.

3 Proposed Conceptual Approach

Before the proposed concept will be presented, short definition of multimodal biometrics systems has to be described. Multimodal safety solutions are a kind of trend in novel approaches to cybersecurity. They use multiple ways to confirm user identity instead of only one. For example, one can easily observe systems based on traditional passwords and unique keys send to the user mobile phone. Then the user has to provide both information before getting an access to the secured data and services. This is a significant example of multimodal safety systems. The user needs to present more than one data (knowledge) by which he will be recognized.

Table 1 Summary of all described research papers

Article	Biometrics trait	Solution
Wei et al. (2004)	Face	FPGA implementation of the AdaBoost algorithm. Acceleration (in comparison to software solution): around 260 times
Khalil-Hani and Eng (2010)	Finger veins	Software implementation and run on Linux RTOS deployed on FPGA evaluation board. No data about acceleration
Eng and Khalil-Hani (2009)	Hand veins	Software implementation and run on Linux RTOS deployed on FPGA evaluation board. No data about acceleration
Van Trieu and Van Cuong (2016)	Face	Hybrid implementation (software and hardware). Communication between two parts with RS232. Acceleration rate more than 4 times
Mohd-Yasin et al. (2004)	Iris	Hybrid implementation (software and hardware). Data from software are moved to FPGA implementation of artificial neural network. No data about acceleration
Pudzs et al. (2013)	Palmprint, Palm veins	FPGA implementation of the whole algorithm. Recognition time equal 0.8 s. No comparison with software-based implementation

Multimodality is also observable in the case of biometrics. It means that instead of only one measurable trait, the system identifies user on the basis of multiple biometrics features. In the literature, one can easily find diversified approaches to these systems. Well-known algorithms are (Yamada and Endoh 2012; Yazdanpanah et al. 2010; Raghavendra et al. 2010). In Yamada and Endoh (2012), the authors proposed to use fingerprints and palm veins while in Yazdanpanah et al. (2010) face, ear and gait biometrics are used. What is interesting in Raghavendra et al. (2010) is that the authors proposed to implement multimodal biometrics system based on hand veins and palmprint. In fact, some time ago, it was claimed that multimodal biometrics systems should consist of at least one physiological trait (that can guarantee high recognition results) and at least one behavioral (e.g., keystroke dynamics) that will play a supporting role for the main trait. However, these systems were really hard to use. It was clearly impossible to collect both traits at the same moment. It is why most of real multimodal biometrics systems are based on at least two physiological traits. Moreover, it was proven that multimodal biometrics systems can guarantee higher accuracy level in recognition than the solutions based on only one measurable feature.

One mandatory thing which system architects should keep in mind is that this system has to be easy to use and all features should be collected really fast. Neither of users would like to use the system that does not provide short time and easiness of sample collection. The authors also though about both these features during system modeling.

The proposed conceptual approach consists of three measurable traits: fingerprint, hand geometry and hand veins. Each of them was selected because of easiness of collection as well as high distinguishability. The concept of the system is presented in Fig. 1.

During previous research, the authors also implemented diversified approaches to biometrics recognition. Our experiences are based on recognition algorithms that use fingerprints (Szymkowski and Saeed 2019), finger veins (Szymkowski and Saeed 2018) and finger geometry (Szymkowski and Saeed 2020). Currently, collected samples are presented in Figs. 2 and 3. In this approach, the authors would like to propose usage of hand veins and hand geometry instead of the same features collected from finger.

The whole system will consist of four main modules. The first of them is related to fingerprint. At the beginning, it will collect sample. In this case, the authors would like to use currently available fast fingerprint scanners or work under their own implemented with FPGA technology. Then collected sample will be moved to preprocessing module in which all unnecessary data will be removed as well as all needed features will be marked. In the last stage (on the basis of final preprocessed sample), feature vector will be generated.

Similar concept will be implemented in the case of hand geometry and hand veins. However, the authors would like to create their own device by which both of these features will be collected. On the basis of previous experiences, the authors will consider specialized camera (for hand geometry collection) and infrared LEDs by which all veins will be clearly visible. Moreover, the authors think that it is possible to collect all three measurable traits simultaneously. It means that fingerprint scanner will also be integrated into proposed device. The concept of the device is presented in Fig. 4.

After generation of all three feature vectors, all of them will be send to decision algorithm implemented with FPGA. The authors considered well-known convolutional neural networks as well as other recognition methods (e.g., Supporting Vector Machines—SVM). This part of the system will be implemented with VHDL programming language.

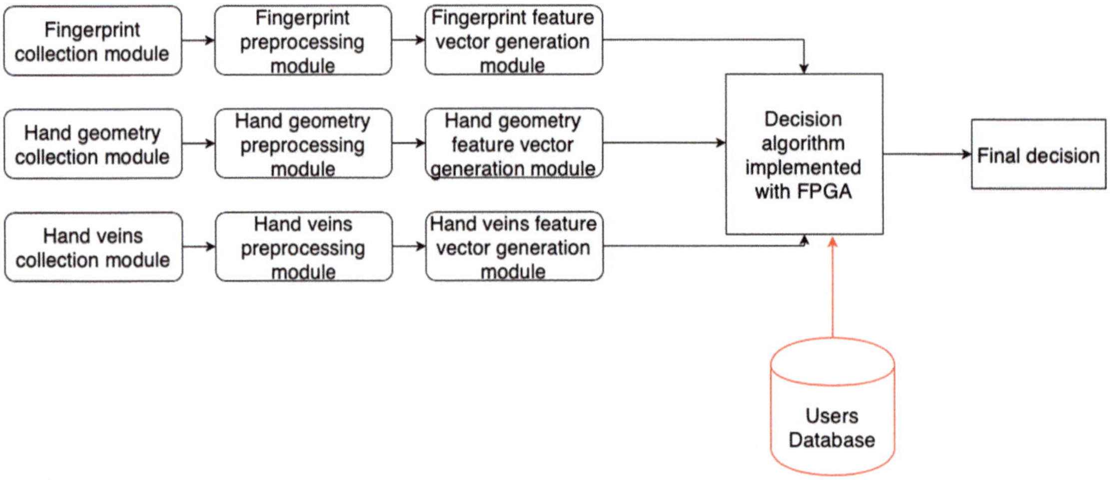

Fig. 1 Concept of the multimodal biometrics system based on FPGA implementations

Fig. 2 Currently collected samples: finger veins (**a**) and finger geometry (**b**)

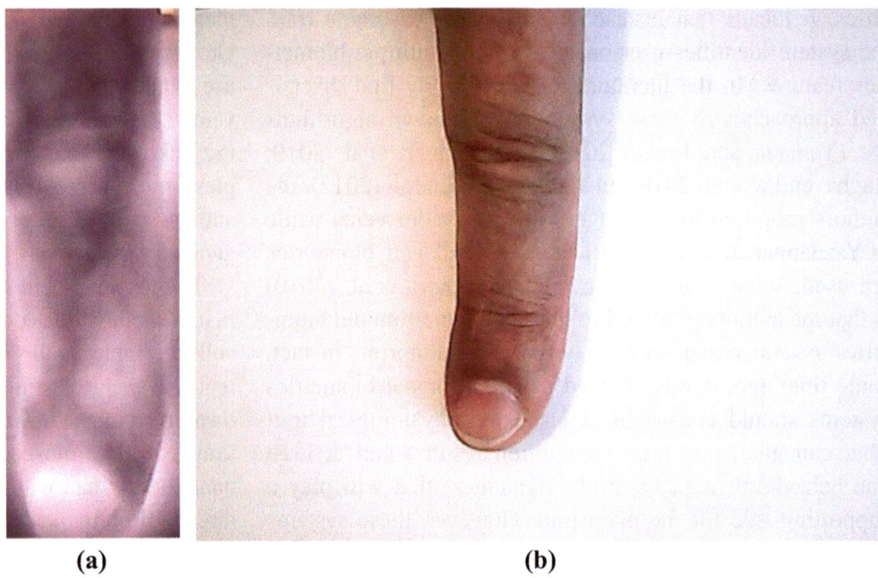

Fig. 3 Currently collected sample—fingerprint

The authors consider two main approaches to implementation of the proposed system. One of them is connected with hybrid way (PC+FPGA), and the second one is connected with FPGA only. Both solutions have their advantages and disadvantages. However, in both cases, the authors will also analyze possibilities to secure communication. It means that the multimodal system should be resistant to eavesdropping (e.g., with novel Bluetooth sniffers) as well as illegal connection to the device. The authors will carefully analyze all ports that should be enabled or disabled. For example, all debug ports will be turned off.

The next idea that has to be considered is connected with data encryption. In the proposed system, all significant information (as collected samples or feature vectors) will not be provided in the explicit form. The authors would like

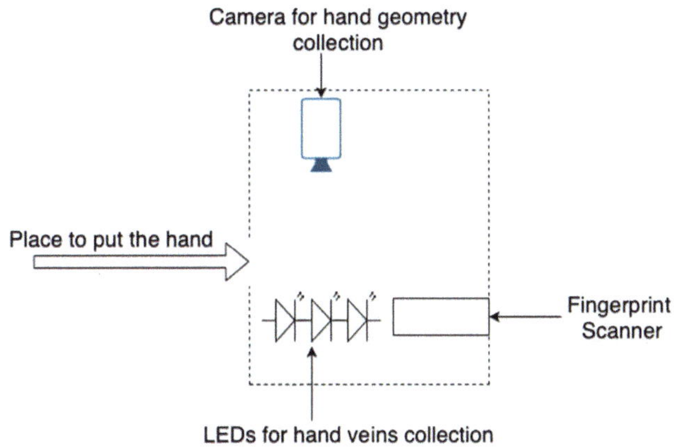

Fig. 4 Scheme of the proposed device

to cipher all data. In this case, two possible solutions are considered—symmetric [e.g., AES (Pitchaiah et al. 2012)] and asymmetric [e.g., RSA (Zhou and Tang 2011; Preetha and Nithya 2013)] form. Moreover, the authors would like to implement encryption algorithm with hardware implementation (VHDL programming language).

The final idea that also will be considered is a communication between our device and end application with Bluetooth transmission technology. It can be implemented with Bluetooth Low Energy (BLE) (developer.android). It means that the administrator can check the vital condition of the device—additional sensors placed inside the device will generate proper information that will be send via Bluetooth. It will allow to observe whether someone does not try to intercept the signals send inside the device. This solution will also increase the safety level for created hardware.

The proposed project, described in this subchapter, considers not only the algorithms that can be used but also some additional procedures by which the safety of the device can be increased. It is connected with the fact that nowadays diversified techniques are available for "eavesdrop" the hardware and obtain significant information connected with the way how it works.

4 Final Remarks

During the state-of-the-art analysis that was a significant part of the conducted research, the authors observed that it is clearly possible to create two approaches to biometrics and FPGA. The first of them is based on implementation only with FPGA (and VHDL programming language), while the second one is based on communication between PC and FPGA development board. In both cases, the authors should consider how to make hardware safer. In this case, the authors think about diversified illegal ways to analyze and modify signals send inside the device.

Moreover, the authors think that their multimodal biometrics approach can be implemented in both ways. It is significant to implement it in both ways and compare whether it is possible to obtain the same accuracy results but in shorter time. Analyzed research papers shows that it is possible to reach this goal.

FPGA is a technology that allows programmer to create hardware implementation of his algorithms or ideas. The conducted research has shown that this technology is used even in the novel approaches to biometrics. An undoubted advantage of FPGA (and VHDL as programming language for this technology) is decreasing the time needed for processing as well as easiness of implementation. The device that the authors described in the subchapter number 3 can be created only with FPGA. It will allow the user to have a completely secure (from hardware) solution that can be used in real environment.

5 Future Work

The authors current work is to implement all algorithms (in their novel forms) described in the third subchapter with software and hardware programming languages—Java and FPGA, respectively. It will allow to create real comparison between both approaches (software and hardware)—accuracy, processing time and samples quality after each stage will be taken into account. Moreover, the authors still are working on the creation of one fully automated device by which all data will be collected simultaneously. Currently available embedded systems are also taken into account.

In the nearest future, the authors will endeavor to make the sample collection (of each trait) available to all interested researchers.

Acknowledgements This work was supported partially by grant S/WI/3/2018 and WI/WI/2/2019 from Białystok University of Technology and funded with resources for research by the Ministry of Science and Higher Education in Poland.

References

Bolle, R.M., J. Connell, S. Pankanti, N.K. Ratha, A.W. Senior. 2004. Guide to biometrics. Springer. ISBN 978-1-4757-4036-3

Choromański, M., T. Grześ, P. Hońko. 2019. Two FPGA devices in the problem of finding minimal reducts. In *Proceedings of Computer Information Systems and Industrial Management. 18th International Conference, CISIM 2019, Belgrade, September 19–21, 2019, Springer Lecture Notes in Computer Science*, ed. K. Saeed, R. Chaki, V. Janev, 410–420.

Eng, P.C., Khalil-Hani, M. 2009. FPGA-based embedded hand vein biometric authentication system. In *Proceedings of 2009 TENCON—2009 IEEE Region 10 Conference*, Singapore, 23–26 Jan 2009, 1-5.

Khalil-Hani, M., P.C. Eng. FPGA-based embedded system implementation of finger veins biometrics. In *Proceedings of 2010 IEEE Symposium on Industrial Electronics and Applications*, Penang, Malaysia, 3–5 Oct 2010, 700–705.

Mohd-Yasin, F., A.L. Tan, M.I. Reaz. The FPGA prototyping of iris recognition for biometric identification employing neural network. In *Proceedings of 2004 IEEE 16th International Conference on Microelectronics*, Tunis, Tunisia, 6–8 Dec 2004, 458–461.

Pitchaiah, M., P. Daniel, Praveen. 2012. Implementation of advanced encryption standard algorithm. *International Journal of Scientific & Engineering Research* 3(3): 1–6.

Preetha, M., and M. Nithya. 2013. A study and performance analysis of RSA algorithm. *International Journal of Computer Science and Mobile Computing* 2 (6): 126–139.

Pudzs, M., R. Fuksis, R. Ruskuls, T. Eglitis, A. Kadikis, M. Greitans. 2013. FPGA based palmprint and palm vein biometric system. In *Proceedings of 2013 IEEE International Conference on the BIOSIG Special Interest Group*, Darmstadt, Germany, 5–6 Sept 2013.

Raghavendra, R., M. Imran, A. Rao, G. Hemantha Kumar. 2010. Multimodal biometrics: Analysis of Handvein and Palmprint Combination used for Person Verification. In *Proceedings of IEEE 2010 3rd International Conference on Emerging Trends in Engineering and Technology*, Goa, India, 19–21 Nov 2010, 526–530.

Saeed, K., and T. Nagashima. 2012. Biometrics and Kansei engineering. Springer. ISBN 978-1-4614-5608-7

Szymkowski, M., K. Saeed. 2018. Finger veins feature extraction algorithm based on image processing methods. In *Proceedings of Computer Information Systems and Industrial Management. 17th International Conference, CISIM 2018, Olomouc, September 27–29, 2018, Springer Lecture Notes in Computer Science*, vol. 11127, ed. K. Saeed, W. Homenda, 80–91.

Szymkowski, M., K. Saeed. 2019. Fingerprint feature extraction with artificial neural network and image processing methods. In *Advances in Soft and Hard Computing, Springer Advances in Intelligent Systems and Computing*, vol. 889, ed. J. Pejaś et al., 86–97.

Szymkowski, M., K. Saeed. 2020. A novel approach to human recognition based on finger geometry. In *Advanced Computing and Systems for Security*, vol. 10", *Springer Advances in Intelligent Systems and Computing*, vol. 996, ed. R. Chaki et al., 57–69.

Van Trieu, V., N. Van Cuong. 2016. PC and FPGA design for face recognition system using Hidden Markov Model. In *Proceedings of 2016 IEEE International Conference on Electronics, Information and Communications, Da Nang*, Vietnam, 27–30 Jan 2016.

Wei, Y., X. Bing, C. Chareonsak. 2004. FPGA implementation of AdaBoost algorithm for detection of face biometrics. In *Proceedings of 2004 IEEE International Workshop on Biomedical Circuits and Systems*, Singapore, 1–3 Dec 2004, 17–20.

Yamada, S., T. Endoh. 2012. Evaluation of independence between palm vein and fingerprint for multimodal biometrics. In *Proceedings of 2012 BIOSIG—Proceedings of the International Conference of Biometrics Special Interest Group*, Darmstadt, Germany, 6–7 Sept 2012.

Yazdanpanah, A.P., K. Faez, R. Amirfattahi. 2010 Multimodal biometric system using face, ear and gait biometrics. In *Proceedings of IEEE 10th International Conference on Information Science, Signal Processing and their Applications (ISSPA 2010)*, Kuala Lumpur, Malaysia, 10–13 May 2010, 251–254.

Zhou, X., X. Tang. 2011. Research and implementation of RSA algorithm for encryption and decryption. In *IEEE Proceedings of 2011 6th International Forum on Strategic Technologies*, Harbin, Heilongjiang, 22–24 Aug 2011.

https://www.elprocus.com/different-types-biometric-sensors/. Accessed 10 Dec 2019.

https://www.xilinx.com/products/silicon-devices/fpga/what-is-an-fpga.html. Accessed 11 Dec 2019.

https://ieeexplore.ieee.org/Xplore/home.jsp. Accessed 02 Nov 2019.

https://link.springer.com. Accessed 02 Nov 2019.

https://developer.android.com/guide/topics/connectivity/bluetooth-le. Accessed 30 Dec 2019.

Correction to: ICT for Engineering & Critical Infrastructures

Asma Salman and Assem Tharwat

Correction to:
Chapters 1 and 5 in: A. Salman and A. Tharwat (eds.), *ICT for Engineering & Critical Infrastructures*, Advances in Science, Technology & Innovation,
https://doi.org/10.1007/978-3-031-49309-6

The original version of this book was published with the incorrect affiliation of the author "Marwan Al-Akaidi" in Chapters 1 and 5. The book and the chapters have been updated with the changes.

The updated versions of these chapters can be found at
https://doi.org/10.1007/978-3-031-49309-6_1,
https://doi.org/10.1007/978-3-031-49309-6_5

© The Author(s), under exclusive license to Springer Nature Switzerland AG 2024

A. Salman and A. Tharwat (eds.), *ICT for Engineering & Critical Infrastructures*,
Advances in Science, Technology & Innovation, https://doi.org/10.1007/978-3-031-49309-6_8

MIX
Papier aus verantwortungsvollen Quellen
Paper from responsible sources
FSC® C105338

If you have any concerns about our products,
you can contact us on
ProductSafety@springernature.com

In case Publisher is established outside the EU,
the EU authorized representative is:
Springer Nature Customer Service Center GmbH
Europaplatz 3, 69115 Heidelberg, Germany

Printed by Libri Plureos GmbH
in Hamburg, Germany